Praise for *Reconsider the Lilies*

"Thompson gives us a thoughtful and candid look at the dangers and inadequacies of Christian environmentalism when it does not take seriously the various and rich ways in which peoples of color see a technicolor creation that we must save. His anti-oppressive Christian environmentalism calls us to cast a wide vision for transformative ways of knowing that embrace a deeply incarnational theology—one that throws open the doors of typical Christian environmentalism to cherish a world of humans and more-than-humans in order to save us all."

—Emilie M. Townes, University Distinguished Professor of Womanist Ethics and Society and Gender and Sexuality Studies, Vanderbilt University Divinity School; author of *Womanist Ethics and the Cultural Production of Evil*

"In a clear and forthright voice, Thompson explains how whiteness has distorted Christian environmentalism. Then, listening well to decolonial and anti-racist voices, he constructs helpful pathways toward an anti-oppressive theological environmentalism. An important book!"

—Willis Jenkins, Hollingsworth Professor of Ethics, University of Virginia

RECONSIDER
THE LILIES

RECONSIDER THE LILIES

Challenging Christian
Environmentalism's
Colonial Legacy

Andrew R. H. Thompson

FORTRESS PRESS
MINNEAPOLIS

To Leigh, Cabell, and Cullen.

Contents

Acknowledgments

To the many people who contributed to the writing of this book, I am deeply grateful. David Chavez, Collin Cornell, Carla Roland Guzmán, Chris Tirres, and Tyler Tully all read portions of the text and offered immensely helpful feedback. In addition, Cathleen Bascom, Christopher Carter, Peter Gray, Laura James, Willis Jenkins, Melanie Mullen, and Aaron Stauffer all provided timely insights. As always, I gained much from exchanges with students, especially "Environmental Ethics" classes in 2020 and 2022. This work would not have been possible without the support of Neil Alexander, Nancy Berner, and Jim Turrell. I am thankful to Ryan Hemmer at Fortress Press for his excellent work throughout the process. And I am very grateful to my wife, Leigh Preston, for her careful eye and thoughtful attention, for introducing me to ideas that were of decisive importance, and for her constant support.

Introduction: Tree of Life

In the chapel on the campus where I teach stands an unusual representation of a tree. Its curving, almost fluid branches appear like any other (except that they reach out in the shape of a cross). Its leaves, however, are more unusual. They are multicolored, not like autumn leaves but rather every color of the rainbow: purple, yellow, red, blue. Each leaf bears a large black circle surrounded by a field of white. Closer inspection reveals that the leaves are, in fact, eyes.

In the traditional Ethiopian style on which the artist drew, eyes symbolize holiness. They can also represent angels, based on biblical texts that describe heavenly attendants as covered in eyes. This eye-covered tree is the work of Bronx-based artist Laura James. It develops the artistic motif of the tree of life, a motif that connects the cross with the tree of life named in the Genesis account of the Garden of Eden, and, beyond that, with the archetypal tree of many religious and mythical traditions. By incorporating the angelic eyes, this tree also invokes the rich, anti-imperial imagination of apocalyptic literature.

The tree is the back of the crucifix that stands at the front of the chapel. Because of its position, the eyes look out through a wall of glass onto the bald cypress, black gum, and northern red oak trees behind the chapel, while Christ on the cross gazes toward the congregation. The body of Jesus on the cross is just as striking as the angel-eyed tree. Christ has dark brown skin, with black hair and a beard. He stands upright, dark eyes wide open, flanked by dark-skinned representations of Mary and John. Angels with dark faces and golden wings fly at his hands and above his head. All of this is rendered in bold colors and clear black outlines.

The seminary commissioned James to create this piece to replace a carved crucifix that portrayed a European-looking, lily-white Jesus hanging, head down, on the arms of the cross. This change was part of an ongoing effort by the seminary, and the university of which it is a part, to acknowledge its history of racism and to move toward reconciliation. My institution, the University of the South, was founded just before the Civil War to educate the young men of the South and to preserve Southern culture: "the University was the only institution of higher education designed from the start to represent, protect, and promote the South's civilization of bondage; and launched expressly for the slaveholding society of the South."[1]

In many ways, this vibrant, colorful crucifix embodies the questions that motivate this book. The representation of Christ as a person of color carries profound significance. Theologian Kelly Brown Douglas argues that representing Christ as Black "indicates his deep and personal identification with people of color as they suffer the pain, heartache, and death exacted on them by the insidiousness of white supremacist culture."[2] But this representation also issues a call to deconstruct and resist that culture in all its forms. What does it mean for a predominantly white institution—an institution originally founded to preserve the structures of white supremacy—to hear and respond to that call? What is the relationship between the dark-skinned depiction of Christ on one side of the crucifix and the tree of life represented on the back? How might this rich symbol, simultaneously ecological and apocalyptic, express opposition to white supremacy?

These are the questions I explore in this book. Our relationship with creation is intimately connected to our relationships with other humans, and our alienation from one another is also our alienation

---

1 "Research Summary," The University of the South, accessed May 14, 2022, https://new.sewanee.edu/roberson-project/learn-more/research-summary/.

2 Kelly Brown Douglas, *The Black Christ: 25th Anniversary Edition* (Maryknoll: Orbis, 2021), xxi.

from the more-than-human world. The suffering taken up by the Black Christ includes the suffering of the earth, and the communion that this Christ represents is a communion that encompasses the whole of creation. But we cannot understand the depths of this communion without first understanding how whiteness has shaped many Christians' relationships with creation, and then working to establish new relationships. This is the task of this book. Before outlining more fully how I intend to undertake this task, I want to say something about my motivation for writing.

I initially came to environmental ethics from an interest in social ethics. My first book examined the social discourses and ideologies at play in the debate around mountaintop removal coal mining in my home region of Appalachia. I was drawn to the issue because of the ways the practice devastated the health and economies of communities while it was destroying ecosystems. In my research, I considered how that debate drew on social constructions of wilderness and nature and deployed ideas about which experiences of the environment were legitimate. I examined the long history of constructing Appalachians as both an inferior class of people and as a romanticized ideal, "our contemporary ancestors," and the ways these stereotypes were exploited in various ways in that debate.[3]

Without equating constructions of Appalachian identity and the environment with ideologies of racism and colonialism, some similar dynamics are at work. Mainstream Christian environmentalism, I will argue, privileges white conceptions of the natural world, based on similar narratives about who does or does not belong in it, about whose experiences count. Often the same paradoxical combination of romanticism and exclusion occurs, particularly regarding Native Americans.

Theologians and ethicists of color have been drawing attention to these oppressive dynamics in environmental theology and other areas of theology for many decades. These voices have become more

---

3 Allen Batteau, *The Invention of Appalachia*, The Anthropology of Form and Meaning (Tucson: University of Arizona Press, 1990), 186.

prominent and more urgent in recent years, as episodes of violence against communities of color have drawn more attention—including environmental violence, like the construction of the Dakota Access Pipeline in North and South Dakota, and the proposed construction of gigantic plastics plants in the industrial corridor known as "cancer alley" in Louisiana. My motivation in this book is to learn from decolonial, Black, womanist, *mujerista*, Latinx, and other scholars who speak from the perspectives of oppressed communities what predominantly white Christian institutions can do to eradicate—or at least minimize—the whiteness at the roots of our environmental efforts.

As I serve on committees, teach classes, and speak at churches about creation care and environmental justice, it is evident that many communities are becoming more aware of the need for critical examination of the prejudices and exclusion that continue to characterize our institutions and our efforts. At the same time, we all (I include myself) have blind spots. Churches may not notice that a panel of environmental speakers is all white, or they may include a person of color only to speak about narrow issues of environmental racism. Committees may similarly be made up of all white members, or they may alternatively treat members of color as if they are invited guests. Groups may view antiracism work as important, but a distraction from the more urgent work of environmental conservation. In Chapter 2, we will see, from ethicist Traci West, further examples of how predominantly white communities may unwittingly exclude people of color. Candid, difficult conversations are necessary, characterized more by listening than by speaking. This book is an attempt to initiate some of those conversations.

My central claim in this book is that Christian environmentalism is characterized by whiteness—that is, by a pervasive privileging of typically white concerns and white experiences of nature. One way that this gets expressed is in the mistaken idea that environmental advocacy and activism can avoid questions of race or class, or questions of political and economic inequality. As I noted above, and as I will discuss further, political, economic, and social power are mediated through the environment. Environmental harms reflect and exacerbate existing societal inequalities and oppressions. Any Christian environmentalism that does not explicitly concern itself with the political and social implications of environmental issues perpetuates white privilege.

Yet the whiteness of Christian environmentalism extends beyond just its areas of concern. To confront this whiteness effectively and move toward a new perspective (what I identify as anti-oppressive Christian environmentalism), we must address the biases deep in our theology and our ways of knowing. For this reason, I will propose an approach that focuses on new ways of imagining and enacting human and more-than-human relationships in a community that extends across the boundaries forged by whiteness. I describe this community as the eco-political body of Christ.

Chapter 1 prepares the soil for this project by providing some key background and vocabulary. I will describe the models Christians have used to understand their responsibility for creation, and explain what I mean by "mainstream Christian environmentalism" and why it is the focus of this book. The critique here assumes a particular conception of whiteness as a socially constructed category; I will explain that conception as well, along with the postcolonial and decolonial approaches that set out to subvert whiteness. Rather than simply being a definition of terms—though that is important—this work of preparation already begins to demonstrate the assumptions and implications involved in our framing of environmental issues. Concepts that seem self-evident (like race) or neutral (like nature) are seen to be more complicated than we think.

I explore the whiteness of Christian environmentalism in Chapter 2. I will describe how the concerns and experiences of communities of color have been systematically excluded from mainstream environmentalism, both secular and Christian. This exclusion is not simply an unfortunate oversight but is expressive of a deeper privileging of a white perspective—what one author identifies as the "white environmentalist frame."[4] I will flesh out this notion with reference to four specific assumptions: a conception of justice that is either weak or overly general; a view of science as apolitical; a focus on the natural world as wilderness; and a reliance on a narrow account of creation. These assumptions reflect the whiteness of green Christianity.

The problem, however, runs deeper than misplaced emphases or narrow interpretations; it is embedded in our theological foundations themselves. Chapter 3 will therefore investigate how this whiteness of green Christianity reflects deeper theological problems. It will be less specifically environmental than other chapters, focusing instead on more fundamental theological questions. Whiteness represents such a profound distortion of our theology that we might speak of whiteness as idolatry. This distortion is exemplified in the doctrine of discovery, a set of legal and theological claims that has provided justification for oppression and the expropriation of land since the fifteenth century. My goal in discussing the doctrine of discovery is not historical but rather ideological and theological, to view it as one particularly clear example of the confluence of white supremacy and theology. The ideas enshrined in the doctrine of discovery establish a doctrine of salvation centered on the construction of whiteness: peoples' capacity to be saved is a function of their place on a racial scale that has whiteness at the top. This doctrine is idolatrous in that it replaces Jesus with this notion of whiteness.

As I will point out in Chapter 1, the dynamics of colonialism established by the doctrine of discovery continue to operate, controlling not only people and resources but ways of knowing as well. The theology of whiteness is similarly made possible by controlling knowledge: only certain forms of knowledge are seen as legitimate, and only certain groups are allowed to produce such knowledge. This production of knowledge serves to support the construction of

---

4 Christopher Carter, "Blood in the Soil: The Racial, Racist, and Religious Dimensions of Environmentalism," in *The Bloomsbury Handbook of Religion and Nature: The Elements*, ed. Laura Hobgood and Whitney Bauman, Bloomsbury Handbooks in Religion (London: Bloomsbury Academic, 2018), 47–48.

whiteness by presenting it as objective fact rather than an ideological claim. Resisting the theological whiteness at the root of Christian environmentalism requires cultivating diverse ways of knowing that emerge from cracks or spaces within the dominant models. I will turn to the perspectives of decolonial theologians and philosophers, particularly queer Chicana feminist writer Gloria Anzaldúa, to explore some of these ways of knowing "in the gaps." These ways of knowing are transgressive in the literal sense of crossing boundaries—in this case, the boundaries whiteness creates among human beings, and between humans and the more-than-human world. The philosophy known as pragmatism will also provide helpful insights to give shape to this knowing in the gaps.

Building on these suggestions of transgressive ways of knowing, Chapter 4 will begin to develop theological foundations for an anti-oppressive Christian environmentalism. We will consider three biblical and theological themes that are transgressive in this way: apocalyptic literature, the nature poetry of the Song of Songs, and the doctrine of incarnation. Ideas of apocalypse are pervasive in environmental writing as human beings reckon with the catastrophic scale of environmental changes. These images have become even more prevalent since the beginning of the COVID-19 pandemic. Yet apocalypse signifies more than just the end of the world. Properly understood, apocalypse means revelation or unveiling, and biblical apocalypse really represents the revelation of a transcendent reality behind and in the events of history. This kind of imagination can motivate political strategies of resistance and pluralism. The Song of Songs expresses a similarly rich imagination of the world, one where boundaries blur between human, plant, and animal; between reality and metaphor; and between literary genres. Like the mythical images of apocalyptic literature, the intimate scenes of the Song of Songs can also be a part of ways of knowing and imagining that resist colonial domination.

The incarnation is arguably the central doctrine of Christian faith; it is also perhaps the most transgressive, crossing the boundaries between human and divine, between the universal and the particular.

The idea of deep incarnation views the incarnation as an event where God takes on not only human flesh but the flesh of all creation. In light of this conception, I will suggest a theology of incarnate ecological community, a sense of relationship in which the boundaries are blurred between human and more-than-human, between spirit and matter, and between transcendence and immanence. This community is the eco-political body of Christ.

Incarnating this body is a demanding task. The roots of whiteness run deep, and challenging them and developing new imaginations takes practice. It requires action, repetition, and habituation in new ways of knowing and relating to one another, and to our more-than-human kin. Chapter 5 will articulate three sets of practices that I believe are necessary to this task. First, liturgy is public practice that gathers community and transforms imaginations. Liturgies can gather humans across boundaries of space and time, including those boundaries imposed by whiteness. But in order to do this, our liturgies and worshipping communities will have to be rethought and reconnected with their roots in creation and deep human community. Second, solidarity is a notion that encompasses practices that embody and enact the deep connections among us. Practices of bioregionalism, which foster connections with particular places and ecosystems, and commoning, which creates cooperative structures of land use and decision-making, are examples of practices of solidarity. Broad-based community organizing also offers specific practices for gathering communities of solidarity, such as relational meetings and the constructive use of anger.

Finally, the concept of ecological reparations can name the concrete actions necessary to begin to overcome whiteness and gather eco-political community across boundaries. Ecological reparations recognize that slavery and colonialism leave scars not only on the political society but also on the land itself, scars that must be repaired if right relationship is to be established. These reparations can be realized in several ways. Land restitution—returning the land to its Indigenous inhabitants—is a necessary part of this practice. But it can also include broader economic reforms and efforts to divest from fossil fuels and reinvest in communities of color. As a recent book on reparations notes, if slavery and colonialism made the world we inhabit today, reparations require nothing less than a similar act of "worldmaking."[5]

Just as this book began with the image of a tree, it concludes with a reflection on two related trees: the tree of the book of Revelation and the witness tree. Trees represent gathering: they gather nutrients and water in their roots, air and sunlight in their leaves, and bring them together into a concrete ecological community. The two trees of the conclusion gather past and future, human and more-than-human, this world and God's transcendent reality, into an incarnate eco-political community. They represent radical imagination—that is, literally, rooted, getting down to the root. They are images of radical resistance to imperial domination and violence, and testaments to a radically different way of being, one that lives reconciled to God and joined to one another.

---

5 Olúfẹ́mi O. Táíwò, *Reconsidering Reparations* (New York: Oxford University Press, 2022), 67.

CHAPTER 1

Colonized Creation

In July of 2020, Michael Brune, the executive director of the Sierra Club, apologized for the club's history of racial insensitivity.[1] In his article, Brune recounts racist statements made by John Muir, the club's founder and a towering figure in the environmental movement.[2] Muir often characterized Native Americans as pitiful and dirty, and considered that they "seemed to have no right place in the landscape."[3] During his travels in the South, he recorded derogatory comments about Black people he passed. Beyond this, Muir associated with individuals like Henry Fairfield Osborn, who, in addition to being a conservationist, was also a white supremacist and eugenicist (that is, he believed in improving the human race by restricting the reproduction of those deemed "unfit," such as disabled people

---

1 Michael Brune, "Pulling Down Our Monuments," Sierra Club, July 22, 2020, https://www.sierraclub.org/michael-brune/2020/07/john-muir-early-history-sierra-club.

2 Contrary to what was reported, Brune did not formally apologize for Muir's statements or "views." Rather, he wrote, "For all the harms the Sierra Club has caused, and continues to cause, to Black people, Indigenous people, and other people of color, I am deeply sorry," Brune, "Pulling Down Our Monuments"; cf. Associated Press, "Sierra Club Apologizes for Founder John Muir's Racist Views," accessed May 9, 2022, https://www.nbcnews.com/news/nbcblk/sierra-club-apologizes-founder-john-muir-s-racist-views-n1234695.

3 "Sierra Club Apologizes for Founder John Muir's Racist Views."

and people of color). Brune also notes that other early leaders of the Sierra Club were vocal supporters of slavery and the Confederacy and, after the Civil War, of white supremacy and eugenics, and that the club essentially had an unwritten policy of excluding people of color from its membership until at least the 1960s. In addition to recounting the truth of the club's history and apologizing, Brune expresses a commitment to concrete steps intended to address these implicit and explicit biases, including budgeting five million dollars for "long-overdue investments in our staff of color and our environmental and racial justice work."[4]

Unsurprisingly, Brune's article elicited a range of responses, some quite emphatic. The Sierra Club published a representative selection of these responses alongside the original piece. Some of them point out that Muir's views changed over his lifetime—noting, for example, that he expressed more sympathetic views of Native Americans, even describing their cultural values as superior to those of white society. Many object to the notion that the club would disavow its connection to Muir or literally remove his name or likeness from its public communications (the article never suggests such steps, though they are seemingly inferred from the article's title, "Pulling Down Our Monuments," which is apparently meant metaphorically). What most of the critical comments have in common, though, is a sense that the Sierra Club should "stay in its lane," keeping its focus on issues of wilderness conservation—a criticism that Brune anticipates in the article itself. A representative example reads, "Instead of attacking [Muir], you should be working on some of the ways the Sierra Club has deprioritized the goal of preserving wilderness since his time."[5]

Why would the Sierra Club stray from its designated lane of environmental conservation? Why not, as one commenter in Brune's article suggests, "acknowledge the flaws of the past and move on"? Why do the views of past leaders and now-obsolete policies matter today? Because, as Brune notes, the views themselves

---

4 Brune, "Pulling Down Our Monuments."
5 Brune.

have not disappeared, and, more importantly, they are related to a more fundamental principle: "the idea that exploring, enjoying, and protecting the outdoors can be separated from human affairs."[6] Muir's racist remarks, even if they were counterbalanced by other more sympathetic ones, are deeply tied to his fundamental beliefs about wilderness. When he insisted that Native Americans seemed to have no place in the landscape, it was precisely the fantasy of a pristine, untouched wilderness that he had in mind. And it was only by literally removing Native Americans (and their long history of ecological management) from the picture that Muir was able to imagine such a wilderness. If the explicitly racist views of some of its early leaders did not persist, this more basic act of erasure did. The failure to reckon with the racism of the club's past reflects a long-standing belief that issues of environmental care and conservation are not affected by the societal ills of racism and prejudice. This belief is not confined to the past, nor is it confined to the Sierra Club.

The focus of this book is Christian environmentalism and environmental theology. Muir was not an environmental theologian. But his environmental vision is deeply spiritually inflected. Muir is an example of what scholar Bron Taylor describes as "dark green religion": a worldview that holds nature as sacred and deserving of care, but does not speak in explicitly religious terms, and is often critical of established religions.[7] Muir's beliefs were seemingly pantheistic, holding that all creation is divine.[8] He was often a vocal critic of Christianity. He frequently invoked God in his writings, but Taylor views this rhetoric more as a pragmatic appeal to Christians than as evidence of Muir's own beliefs.[9] Notwithstanding his own distance from Christianity, though, Muir has been embraced by Christian environmentalists.

---

6 Brune.

7 Bron Taylor, *Dark Green Religion: Nature Spirituality and the Planetary Future* (Berkeley: University of California Press, 2010).

8 Taylor, *Dark Green Religion*, 62.

9 Taylor, 62.

Most importantly, however, Muir's ideas about nature and wilderness, along with similar ideas from other monumental figures in the environmental movement, have shaped Christian environmentalism. The characteristics and implications of these ideas will be the focus of Chapter 2. From Muir and others, Christian environmentalism has inherited a view of environmental care and stewardship as mostly separate from concerns about social and economic justice, and as primarily concerned with the protection of pristine wild places and landscapes, rather than broken places or places of work.

This view has only recently begun to be dislodged from its central place in mainstream environmentalism, religious and secular. Part of the motivation for writing this book is my own experience serving on different creation care groups made up of committed, well-intentioned, mostly white Christians. Invariably in our deliberations, some version of the sentiment expressed by the commenter above emerges: instead of confronting questions of racial bias and environmental racism, we should focus on our mandate of addressing more properly "environmental" issues, like climate change and wilderness protection. That racism and white supremacy might be at the heart of these environmental issues still seems, to many, incomprehensible.

Such a view can only be maintained by the erasure of Native Americans, Black people, and other people of color, whose histories and experiences of the more-than-human creation demonstrate the intimate connections between environmental harms and the societal ills of racism, colonialism, and white supremacy. It is by now well known that communities of color are disproportionately affected by environmental harms like pollution. This phenomenon is known as environmental racism. Even after adjusting for other variables like wealth or housing, race is the strongest indicator of whether a community is exposed to toxic pollution. The United Church of Christ documented environmental racism in its landmark 1987 report, *Toxic Wastes and Race in the United States,* and when it revisited the same questions in 2007 with *Toxic Wastes and Race at*

Twenty, it found that environmental racism had actually worsened.[10] The later report pointed specifically to several statistics: that at that time, Black children were five times more likely than white children to have lead poisoning; that 46 percent of affordable housing units sat within a mile of factories producing toxic emissions; and that more than 600,000 students at nearly 120,000 schools in five states, largely children of color, attended school within a half mile of a known contaminated waste site.[11]

Hurricane Katrina, which struck New Orleans in 2005, received special attention in the 2007 report. The report notes that both protection during the storm and cleanup after it were unequally distributed according to race. Poor communities of color were less protected before the storm, and after it much of the waste, including potentially toxic waste, was sent to predominantly African American areas.[12]

The example of Hurricane Katrina illustrates that environmental racism applies not only to localized harms like toxic waste but also to global problems like climate change, since hurricanes themselves are made more likely by changes in the global climate. This unequal distribution plays out in a variety of ways. Formerly colonized countries are more likely to experience the effects of climate change, in the present and in the future, than countries that have never been colonized. Within countries, too, effects of climate change like extreme heat affect communities of color disproportionately. The first official climate refugees of the United States were the Isle de Jean Charles Band of the Biloxi-Chitimacha-Choctaw. They were awarded $48 million for relocation when sea-level rise submerged their island

---

10 United Church of Christ Commission for Racial Justice, *Toxic Wastes and Race in the United States*; United Church of Christ Justice and Witness Ministries et al., *Toxic Wastes and Race at Twenty: 1987–2007* (United Church of Christ, 2007).

11 United Church of Christ Justice and Witness Ministries et al., *Toxic Wastes and Race at Twenty*, 4.

12 United Church of Christ Justice and Witness Ministries et al., 124–26.

and, with it, a crucial component of their culture.[13] Other Native American communities' homes are similarly threatened by sea-level rise. Even temperature is unevenly distributed. A study in New York City showed that heatwave deaths were higher in areas with large populations of color than in areas with largely white populations, which had more plants and air conditioners.[14]

These dynamics reproduce the historical imbalances of colonialism, as we will see. But these injustices are only one side of the story. Communities of color are not only environmental victims. The engagement and perspectives of Native American communities, Black communities, and other communities of color with the natural world are shaped by complex histories and experiences different from what have typically been the dominant perspectives. These experiences and perspectives have typically been either neglected or romanticized by mainstream environmentalism. To imagine that environmental thought and action can be separated from these different histories, and from the realities of racism and oppression, is a view that can only come from a position of privilege. It is, I will argue in this book, a view that is fundamentally dependent on a constructed idea of whiteness.

I. MAINSTREAM CHRISTIAN ENVIRONMENTALISM

Whiteness has deep roots in mainstream Christian environmentalism. Beyond just ideas about wilderness and nature, they include fundamental theological beliefs about creation and salvation, and even our most basic ways of knowing. Exposing and dismantling these roots will require more than new ideas or ways of speaking about creation. It will require new ways of thinking, imagining, and being community. It will require the eco-political body of Christ. Later in this chapter, I will explain some of the terms and ideas

---

13 Táíwò, *Reconsidering Reparations*, 64–71, 161–62.
14 Táíwò, 161.

that are integral to my argument (like whiteness, anti-oppressive, colonialism, and decoloniality/decolonization). First, though, I want to present some background about what I am calling mainstream Christian environmentalism.

It becomes less and less necessary to justify Christian concern about environmental issues as increasing numbers of churches recognize care for creation as a central part of their faith. While Christian social movements in the early twentieth century recognized a need to care for creation, sustained attention to environmental crises through words and actions—what we would recognize as Christian environmentalism—did not emerge until the 1960s and 1970s.[15] Through those decades, scholars both within and outside Christianity turned their attention to the environment. A key focus of the discussion was the question of whether Christian theology was irredeemably anthropocentric—that is, centered exclusively on human beings and their needs. The most influential argument in this vein was from historian Lynn White Jr., who argued that Christian anthropocentrism was to blame for environmental crises.[16] Western Christianity, White said, was the most anthropocentric religion the world had seen, particularly in its creation accounts. Through its influence on Western science and technology, this worldview created an attitude that instrumentalized and exploited creation. White's argument has shaped Christian environmental theology for decades, whether to refute his thesis or confirm it.

In the 1970s and 1980s, conferences and groups began to promote not only theological reflection but also organized action around environmental concerns. These groups included the National Council of Churches Eco-Justice Working Group, conferences sponsored by the World Council of Churches, and significant statements from Pope John Paul II, Orthodox Patriarch Bartholomew (often called

---

15 Laurel Kearns, "Ecology and Religious Environmentalism in the United States," in *The Oxford Encyclopedia of Religion in America*, ed. John Corrigan, vol. 2 (New York: Oxford University Press, 2018), 609.

16 Lynn White Jr., "The Historical Roots of Our Ecologic Crisis," *Science* 155, no. 3767 (1967): 1203.

the "green Patriarch"), and the National Association of Evangeli-cals.[17] During this time, the most prominent statements, declarations, and calls to action came from mainline Protestantism (that is, the predominantly white denominations that made up the majority of Protestants in the United States until the mid-twentieth century), Roman Catholicism, and white evangelicalism. This is not to say that nonwhite or other marginalized communities were not engaged in environmental action; as we will see in Chapter 2, it was precisely during these decades that the environmental justice movement was emerging, marching primarily out of houses of worship in communi-ties of color. But for most of the early decades, recognizable Christian environmentalism was mainly associated with these predominantly white institutions, and that perception still holds for many people.[18]

Sociologist Laurel Kearns identifies three broad strands of Christian environmentalism that have proven helpful in tracing its development: stewardship, eco-justice, and creation spirituality.[19] A stewardship ethic is firmly grounded in the Bible, especially the Genesis creation accounts, which give Christians the responsibility to be stewards, caretakers of creation on God's behalf. This tradition frames environmental care as part of a faithful relationship with God, and preserves humans' special place within the plan of creation. For critics, this is cause for concern, particularly when viewed in light of the biblical instructions to "subdue" and "have dominion" over creation (Gen 1:28). Proponents of a stewardship view counter that these terms have to be viewed in the context of the larger creation narrative, which modifies these instructions with the gentler commands to "till and keep" (Gen 2:15), and of God's overall pattern of dominion, which is one

---

17 Laurel Kearns, "Religious Climate Activism in the United States," in *Religion in Environmental and Climate Change: Suffering, Values, Lifestyles*, ed. Dieter Gerten and Sigurd Bergmann (London: Bloomsbury Academic, 2012), 134.

18 Kearns, "Ecology and Religious Environmentalism in the United States," 621.

19 Laurel Kearns, "Saving the Creation: Christian Environmentalism in the United States," *Sociology of Religion* 57, no. 1 (March 1, 1996): 55–70, https://doi.org/10.2307/3712004.

of caring, attentive relationship.[20] This pattern is given new and explicit meaning in Christ, who reshapes lordship as service. For a stewardship approach, environmental crises are seen not as an indictment of the anthropocentrism of Christianity as a whole but rather as the result of humans' failure to attend to their God-given task. This approach tends to be more associated with evangelical Protestantism, including the Evangelical Environmental Network, which formed in the 1990s.[21]

The perspective of eco-justice, which began in the 1970s and gained greater currency with the creation of the Eco-Justice Working Group of the National Council of Churches in 1983, is more prominent among mainline Protestant denominations. It connects the suffering of creation with the suffering of the poor, and thus extends concern for social justice to environmental issues.[22] Theologically, the call to care for creation is grounded in God's overall mission of reconciliation: God is acting to overcome alienation and bring all things into harmony. Human participation in God's mission requires caring for vulnerable humans as well as a vulnerable creation. Like a stewardship approach, the eco-justice perspective frames environmental care as part of right relationship with God. It does so not by setting humans and human responsibility apart from creation, however, but by bringing creation into the sphere of human justice. Because of this inclusive conception of justice, eco-justice has typically been more attentive than alternative approaches to the role played by race and class in environmental problems.[23] This combination, however, has led to tensions that will be explored in Chapter 2.

Creation spirituality is a broad category that takes its basic orientation not from the creation accounts of Genesis but from scientific

---

20 Willis Jenkins, *Ecologies of Grace: Environmental Ethics and Christian Theology* (Oxford and New York: Oxford University Press, 2008), 80–81.

21 Kearns, "Saving the Creation," 59.

22 Jenkins, *Ecologies of Grace*, 62–65.

23 Kearns, "Ecology and Religious Environmentalism in the United States," 611.

accounts of the origin and ultimate end of the universe.[24] Rather than emphasize humans' unique role in creation, it portrays us as simply part of a whole, and as distinctively capable of both self-reflection and great destruction. It finds tools for this holistic vision in mysticism and science. Theologically, it interprets its vision in light of what is sometimes described as the "Cosmic Christ," who restores the whole cosmos in a new creation.[25] Among its eclectic sources, biblical passages like Romans 8:19–22 speak to this theology: "The creation waits with eager longing for the revealing of the children of God . . . the creation will be set free from its enslavement to decay and will obtain the freedom of the glory of the children of God. We know that the whole creation has been groaning together. . . ." This approach appeals mainly to more liberal Protestants, less traditional Roman Catholics, and the unchurched, and in some of its versions, it has a relatively loose relationship with Christian orthodoxy and institutions.

I will return to Kearns's three categories in Chapter 2. This broad tradition, comprising all three approaches, is what I mean by "mainstream Christian environmentalism." This terminology tracks with what has been called "mainstream environmentalism," referring to those secular conservation groups that have similarly failed to recognize their own whiteness.[26] At times, I will also refer to ecotheology, alongside or instead of Christian environmentalism. Where Christian environmentalism encompasses the whole category of advocacy, action, and reflection on environmental issues from a Christian perspective, ecotheology is specifically the theological work—in books, scholarly articles, public statements, and the like— that provides ideological support for Christian environmentalism. The two are closely connected; addressing the blind spots of Christian environmentalism requires attending to its theological foundations.

---

24 Kearns, "Saving the Creation," 60–61.

25 Jenkins, *Ecologies of Grace*, 97.

26 Willis Jenkins, *The Future of Ethics: Sustainability, Social Justice, and Religious Creativity* (Washington, DC: Georgetown University Press, 2013), 203.

It is partly because of its predominance—both in terms of public profile and in terms of general perceptions—that mainstream Christian environmentalism is the focus of this book. I also focus on mainstream Christian environmentalism because it is the tradition within which I work, and with which I am most familiar. As I noted above, I have witnessed the dynamics I trace in this book firsthand. Finally, then, I focus on this tradition because that is where the problem is. This broad category of Christian environmental thought and action remains deeply formed by whiteness.

II. RECONSIDERING THE LILIES: WHITENESS

On May 14, 2022, a white supremacist opened fire at a supermarket in Buffalo, New York, killing ten people and wounding three others. The gunman had written and posted a 180-page manifesto online in which he professed what is known as the "great replacement theory," an ideology that imagines that white people are at risk of losing their culture and privilege because of increasing diversity and immigration.[27] Like earlier violent adherents of this ideology, the shooter also described himself as an "eco-fascist" and portrayed his white supremacy as environmental conscientiousness.[28]

The warped logic behind these claims blames nonwhite immigrants for environmental degradation and sees overpopulation and increased urbanization as the main causes of climate change, associating those, too, with people of color and nonwhite developing countries. This logic, of course, completely ignores the fact that high levels of consumption in wealthy countries contribute far more to climate change than overpopulation, and that migration is increasingly a result of the effects of climate change, rather than a cause, as droughts and sea-level rise create climate refugees. Nonetheless, aspects of this

27 Oliver Milman, "Buffalo Suspect May Be Latest Mass Shooter Motivated by 'Eco-Fascism,'" *The Guardian*, May 17, 2022, https://www.theguardian.com/us-news/2022/may/17/buffalo-shooting-suspect-eco-fascism.
28 Milman, "Buffalo Suspect."

ideology are becoming more common, as right-wing groups in the United States and around the world campaign on ideas of immigrants as "unclean," and on nativist visions of environmental care that are used as justification for restrictive immigration policies.[29]

The ease with which this ideology, in both its extremist and more mainstream forms, is able to co-opt environmental sustainability is troubling, but it should not be surprising. As Brune's article acknowledges, environmental conservation in the United States has been connected with white supremacy from the beginning. While the extremist rhetoric of replacement theory is explicit in its affirmation of these connections, other forms of environmentalism, including Christian environmentalism, have inherited aspects of this legacy as well. The specter of overpopulation, now described in terms of "carrying capacity," still figures prominently in discussions of sustainability, as do, again, images of pristine wilderness.[30] This is not to blame mainstream environmentalism or equate it with extremist rhetoric or violence. It is, however, important to be aware of the assumptions that underlie environmental perspectives and the problematic associations they carry.

Notions like these privilege certain environmental experiences and values associated with whiteness, as I will explain more thoroughly in Chapter 2. In speaking of whiteness, I am not primarily talking about demographics or skin color (though whiteness is secondarily about these things). By saying that mainstream Christian environmentalism is influenced by whiteness, I am not simply saying that it has come mostly from predominantly white institutions (though, again, historically it has). Whiteness is not a neutral biological category, simply a description of skin color, that unfortunately gets corrupted into racism. Rather, whiteness is a social construction

---

29 Milman, "Buffalo Suspect"; S. Lily Mendoza and George Zachariah, "Introduction," in *Decolonizing Ecotheology: Indigenous and Subaltern Challenges*, ed. S. Lily Mendoza and George Zachariah (Eugene, OR: Pickwick Publications, 2022), 4.

30 Jenkins, *The Future of Ethics*, 244–49.

that is, from the very beginning, invested in establishing hierarchies and systems of privilege and oppression.

In the historical context of global colonialism, whiteness was a way of organizing various peoples into one hierarchical system, with Europeans firmly at the top.[31] It is this hierarchy that comes first; the concept of race is mapped onto the categories as a justification after the fact, to establish it as naturally determined. As we will see in Chapter 3, whiteness has always been a theological concept: white Europeans were constructed as superior because they were believed to be spiritually more developed, closer to God, while people of color could be improved (always within the rigid hierarchy of the system) by being brought to Christ and controlled by white people.[32]

Whiteness takes on a distinctive character and significance in the United States, and it is this expression of whiteness that will be central to this book. Whiteness as a construction in the US can be seen most readily in the way different groups—many of whom would today be identified as white—have been seen as falling within and beyond the boundaries of whiteness at different times. In the United States, which was founded on a myth of Anglo-Saxon superiority, whiteness became a category that could sustain that claim of superiority in spite of the fact that it was a nation of immigrants.[33] If the increasingly diverse young nation could no longer maintain its claim of exceptionalism based on its imagined Anglo-Saxon identity, it could fabricate a new category as the basis for that claim. As new immigrants arrived from parts of Europe that were seen as less desirable, they could gain access to privilege by claiming their identity as white and distinguishing themselves from Black people. This process is how ethnicities are constructed.[34]

---

31 Willie James Jennings, *After Whiteness: An Education in Belonging*, illustrated ed. (Grand Rapids, MI: Eerdmans, 2020), 19.

32 Kelly Brown Douglas, *The Black Christ*, 5–6.

33 Kelly Brown Douglas, *Stand Your Ground: Black Bodies and the Justice of God* (Maryknoll, NY: Orbis, 2015), 27–35.

34 Douglas, *Stand Your Ground*, 35.

In this way, from the beginning whiteness has been defined not by skin color but by its opposition to Blackness; that is by who it excludes in order to protect its privileges. It is never a neutral descriptor, but always an exclusive claim of superiority. White supremacy explicitly mobilizes this claim of superiority for (often violent) domination. The idea of superiority, though, is already present within the construction of whiteness itself.[35] And here, too, whiteness is from the start a theological concept: the exceptionalism of the nation's founding was always seen as religious superiority, and the protection of the United States' evangelical Protestant identity was one of the main motivators for the construction of whiteness here.[36]

This is the understanding of whiteness that I draw on in this book. This means that when I describe whiteness as idolatry, for example, or when I seek to challenge whiteness, I am not speaking of white people but rather of the socially constructed category that makes them white, and the subtle (or sometimes not-so-subtle) privileging of white experience that goes with that category. When, in Chapter 2, I describe the whiteness of green Christianity, I am talking not of its demographics but of the assumptions it includes that are part of the construction of whiteness and the protection of its privileges.

This reappraisal of whiteness is what inspires this book's title, which is a play, of course, on Luke 12:27: "Consider the lilies, how they grow: they neither toil nor spin, yet I tell you, even Solomon in all his glory was not clothed like one of these."[37] Lilies are typically thought of as white—indeed, the phrase "lily-white" expresses the purest white (though ironically, the flower referred to in Luke 12:27 is just as likely red).[38] So on one level, the invitation to reconsider the lilies is simply a call to take a close look at the whiteness present in our theologies, and particularly our creation theologies and

---

35 Matt R. Jantzen, *God, Race, and History: Liberating Providence* (Lanham: Lexington Books, 2021), 4.

36 Douglas, *Stand Your Ground*, 35–36.

37 The title was suggested by Ryan Hemmer at Fortress Press.

38 "Strong's Greek: 2918. Κρίνον (Krinon)—a Lily," accessed May 10, 2022, https://biblehub.com/greek/2918.htm.

environmentalism. But this text, and my title, are about more than the image of a single flower, white or not. In the text's broader context, Jesus is teaching his disciples not to occupy themselves with material concerns such as wealth, food, or clothing. Here, first birds and then flowers are used to illustrate the kind of life Jesus seems to be commending: a life dependent on God, unburdened by preoccupation with material goods but lacking nothing necessary. This is clearly an environmental text, even if it is not only that. The life being described here is seemingly one that resists some of the most environmentally destructive attitudes of our day, such as materialism, consumerism, incessant work, and accumulation. The natural world is presented as a teacher of such a life.

At the same time, reconsidering this story from a perspective more critical of whiteness, we might note the privilege inherent in such an interpretation. Consumerism and a work-obsessed lifestyle are pathologies that infect some groups more than others, and a life without unnecessary worry is a luxury that many cannot afford. Furthermore, many authors have pointed out that appeals to personal attitudes and lifestyles neglect the political and systemic nature of environmental crises.[39] An attitude of radical dependence on God's grace is not in itself a solution to ecological crises created by economic and political systems and systemic social evils like racism. Finally, the typical interpretation of this story implicitly trades on ideas of the purity and pristineness of nature that, as we have seen and will see, have historically been problematic.

I am not suggesting that the usual interpretation of this passage is wrong; only that it is incomplete. In short, the reference in the title is an invitation to examine carefully the sometimes-subtle role whiteness often plays in our environmentalism and ecotheologies.

Closely related to the constructed idea of whiteness are some of the other terms I will use in this book, such as decolonial, antiracist, and anti-oppressive. The notion of decoloniality emerges from discourses

---

39 Rachel K. Taber-Hamilton, "When Creation Is Sacred: Restoring the Indigenous Jesus," *Anglican Theological Review* 103, no. 2 (2021): 168.

of postcolonial thought. Postcolonial thought "occurs in the wake of formal colonialism and continues through intellectual and political resistance to neocolonialism"—that is, resistance to the political and economic systems that continue to oppress former colonies, even after the end of formal colonialism.[40] In the United States in particular, this involves resisting settler colonialism, the form of colonialism that removed Native Americans forcibly or coercively from their land so that settlers could occupy it, as we still do. Among other things, postcolonial thought examines the ideologies—like whiteness—that continue to exclude and subjugate people on the margins.

Decoloniality is an idea that develops from and in response to postcolonialism. Like postcolonialism, decoloniality resists the dynamics and structures of colonialism that persist today. In contrast to postcolonialism, though, decoloniality insists that colonialism is not past but is a feature of modernity—that is, that the ways that power and knowledge are organized, distributed, and controlled globally continue to perpetuate the oppressive dynamics of the colonial system.[41] Above all, decoloniality therefore puts forward alternative ways of organizing society and alternative ways of knowing that undermine those dynamics. The insights of decoloniality for deconstructing the whiteness of environmental theology will be the focus of Chapter 3.

Antiracism is another project closely linked with decoloniality. Because white supremacy is one of the central narratives of coloniality, and race one of its key ideological categories (especially in the United States), directly challenging the notion of race and its privileging of whiteness is a decolonial project.[42] The goal of this book is

---

40 Sarah Azaransky, "Impossible, Inadequate, and Indispensable: What North American Christian Social Ethics Can Learn from Postcolonial Theory," *Journal of the Society of Christian Ethics* 37, no. 1 (January 1, 2017): 46.

41 Aníbal Quijano, "Coloniality and Modernity/Rationality," *Cultural Studies* 21, no. 2–3 (March 1, 2007): 169, https://doi.org/10.1080/09502380601164353; cf. Walter D. Mignolo and Catherine E. Walsh, *On Decoloniality: Concepts, Analytics, Praxis* (Durham, NC: Duke University Press, 2018), 111, 141.

42 Christopher Carter, *The Spirit of Soul Food: Race, Faith, and Food Justice* (Urbana: University of Illinois Press, 2021), 11–17.

to offer suggestions toward an antiracist and decolonial Christian environmentalism.

However, while part of this project of resisting coloniality and whiteness involves seeing the ideological connections between antiracist and decolonial work and deconstructing these patterns of thought, colonialism and decoloniality are not only about ideology. It is important not to lose sight of the material realities of colonization and the radical material demands of decolonization. In an influential article, Eve Tuck and K. Wayne Yang warn against understanding decolonization as a metaphor.[43] They argue that different forms of colonialism are not interchangeable, and that the settler colonialism of the United States involves "a total appropriation of Indigenous life and land," and the rupture of indigenous relationships to land.[44] Conflating different forms of colonization and decolonization, or conflating antiracism with decolonization, neglects the realities of different forms of oppression. "Decolonization," say Tuck and Yang, "doesn't have a synonym."[45]

Even more importantly, we make decolonization a metaphor when we focus exclusively on ideological deconstruction and consciousness building. These moves, according to Tuck and Yang, are crucial to reducing the harm caused by white supremacy, but they are not the same as decolonization: "decolonization requires the repatriation of Indigenous land and life."[46] I will argue in Chapter 5 that conceptual or imaginative shifts are insufficient, and that actual repatriation of land and concrete reparations are necessary practices for Christian environmentalism.

By challenging the whiteness of Christian environmentalism, I hope to describe an environmentalism that is antiracist and decolonial, one that actively and concretely contributes to the goals of these projects—again, distinctive goals, but goals that both require the dismantling of

---

43 Eve Tuck and K. Wayne Yang, "Decolonization Is Not a Metaphor," *Decolonization: Indigeneity, Education, and Society* 1, no. 1 (September 8, 2012): 1–40.
44 Tuck and Yang, "Decolonization Is Not a Metaphor," 5.
45 Tuck and Yang, 3.
46 Tuck and Yang, 21.

whiteness. In order to avoid the impression that this work is sufficient to antiracism or decolonization, though, or that antiracism and decolonization are somehow interchangeable, I will describe my goal as an anti-oppressive Christian environmentalism.[47] What I mean by this is a Christian environmentalism that actively opposes all systems and ideologies of oppression. This is an environmentalism that supports the goals of antiracism and decolonization by challenging whiteness, but is not sufficient to, or identifiable with, either of those projects.

III. HUMAN, NONHUMAN, AND MORE-THAN-HUMAN

Even as Christians have become more aware of the centrality of creation care to their faith, how we talk about that commitment has become ever more complicated, as all of the traditional terminology seems inadequate. "Creation" is appropriately holistic, encompassing everything, but for this reason it is often not specific enough. Humans and animals are part of creation, but so too are plants, the seas, the sky, and the whole cosmos. On the other hand, words like "nature" and "environment" are more specific, but they reinforce the problematic divide between humans and everything else. When used to talk about animals, plants, and nonliving features of the natural world, these terms rely on a belief that humans are distinctive, unique, set apart from all other species and categories, and implicitly center the human as the primary category (this, again, is referred to as "anthropocentrism"). The term "nonhuman" is even worse in this regard, in that it defines other species and beings based solely on the fact that they are not human. Here the human/other divide subsumes all other characteristics. Moreover, the same conceptual move that divides humans from nonhuman animals has historically been used to establish human hierarchies, categorizing some humans as more akin to animals.[48] On the other side, terms like these suggest that

---

47 Cf. Carter, *The Spirit of Soul Food*, 11.
48 Carter, 128–29.

the "nature" or "environment" being talked about is unified, perhaps harmonious, and, above all, unaffected by human impacts. As we have seen already, from John Muir to replacement theory, these fantasies of a pristine natural world have been used to oppress and exclude those who are believed not to belong in the "landscape."

In any case, in today's world these distinctions are unsustainable. Humans have never been separate from the rest of creation, of course, but human impacts have now become so pervasive that some scholars have begun to speak of a new geological epoch, the Anthropocene, in which the dominant driver of change is human action.[49] Arguably no part of creation is unaffected by human actions. At the same time, we are increasingly aware that our bodies include other species, so that the boundary between a human body and its environment suddenly becomes permeable. Terminologies that reinforce humans' imagined separation from the rest of creation are inaccurate at best and, as I will argue elsewhere in this book, ecologically and socially harmful at worst.

In this context, one alternative that has emerged to talk about all the species and ecosystems besides humans that make up the creation is the term "more-than-human."[50] This way of describing other beings combines several connected ideas. It names other species and systems without making them simply a negation of what is human. It suggests an inescapable relatedness between humans and others; human and more-than-human are dependent upon each other. Yet it also claims that rather than being inferior, those others have qualities that exceed or go beyond those of humans. It recalls the way traditional terminologies have worked by alienating humans from their more-than-human kin, but upends those traditional terminologies by privileging those others.

In this book, I will use the language of creation as the primary theological vocabulary for speaking of the whole collection of species,

---

49 Paul J. Crutzen and Eugene F. Stoermer, "The Anthropocene," *Global Change Newsletter* 41, no. 1 (2000).

50 Joseph Pugliese, *Biopolitics of the More-Than-Human*, Forensic Ecologies of Violence (Durham, NC: Duke University Press, 2020), 3, https://doi.org/10.2307/j.ctv17z84k4.4.

ecosystems, and landscapes. But to refer more specifically to those parts of the creation that are not human, I will rely on the term "more-than-human," with these various inflections in mind. This term remains imperfect, of course, in that it still reflects a distinction between humans and other beings. Some degree of this problem is inevitable, though, since the negotiation of this relationship is a crucial part of what is at issue in this book.

These discussions serve to remind us that terminology matters. Ostensibly neutral terms like "nature" and "environment," or seemingly self-evident categories like race are constructed a certain way. They are, in that sense, not "natural." They do not have to be constructed the way that they are, and typically their construction serves particular interests. Someone usually gains by the way that concepts are constructed and organized. As we will see in Chapter 3, how knowledge is organized and distributed is closely connected to how power is exercised. How we name things is a part of this exercise. What is considered an environmental problem—is housing, for example, an environmental problem?—is often a feature of who defines what we mean by "environmental" and what their experience is. Resources and power then follow from that definition.

When the term "sustainability" is so easily co-opted by white supremacist extremists to justify violence, we are forced to pay close attention to our words and concepts and the associations and histories they carry. This chapter has begun this task, considering the frameworks Christians use to think about their relation to the more-than-human world. I have clarified some of the terms that will be essential for this book, and shown that, in many cases, they are not as self-evident or uncontroversial as we might assume. Rather, many of these terms are sites for ongoing negotiation of meaning. In the chapters that follow, we will continue to probe some of the assumptions typical of mainstream Christian environmentalism and the theological foundations that support them, in order to describe a more anti-oppressive perspective. Chapter 2 considers how several key characteristics of Christian environmentalism are indelibly marked by whiteness.

CHAPTER 2

Green Christianity Is White

I. ENVIRONMENTALISM AND
ENVIRONMENTAL RACISM

In the summer of 1978, a black tanker truck owned by the Ward Transformer Company drove along the highways of North Carolina in the middle of the night, intentionally dripping oil contaminated with the chemical polychlorinated biphenyl (PCB) on the shoulder of the road. Over nearly two weeks, the truck spread 31,000 gallons of the contaminated oil over more than 200 miles of highway. When the pollution was discovered, warning signs were erected along the highways, and the state began making plans to construct a PCB landfill in Warren County, a predominantly African American county, over the opposition of its residents. When the state prepared to haul 10,000 truckloads of PCB-contaminated soil to the landfill in 1982, hundreds of protesters lay down in the trucks' path. The protests, which lasted six weeks, led to more than five hundred arrests.

Although the Warren County protests were unable to stop the landfill (which unsurprisingly failed, dangerously polluting the air and water), they helped launch the environmental justice movement, and they introduced the idea of environmental racism. Environmental justice can be understood as a broad movement of grassroots activism that seeks to expose and resist the ways environmental harms are unequally distributed—that is, the ways environmental problems like air and water pollution disproportionately affect marginalized groups, such as women, impoverished communities, and communities of color. "Environmental racism" is a term that was first coined by organizers of the Warren County protests to indicate that race is a particularly significant factor in the unequal distribution of these environmental harms.

When organizers first uttered this charge, they spoke from the lived experience of this inequality. That experience of environmental racism was given statistical confirmation in 1987 when the United Church of Christ (UCC) released *Toxic Wastes and Race in the United States,* under the leadership of Pastor Benjamin Chavis, who had been one of the organizers in Warren County. The report showed that race was the most significant statistical factor in determining which communities hosted toxic waste facilities, more than income or home value. Three out of five Black and Hispanic Americans lived in a community that housed a closed or abandoned site that posed a threat to both human health and the environment—what the EPA called an "uncontrolled toxic waste site." Environmental racism was now a documented fact.[1] Twenty years later, using improved methodology, *Toxic Wastes and Race at Twenty* confirmed the original finding that "race continues to be an independent predictor of where hazardous wastes are located, and it is a stronger predictor than income, education and other socioeconomic indicators."[2] Further, the report's authors found that the Environmental Protection Agency (EPA), rather than addressing environmental racism, "has been hostile to environmental justice and environmental justice principles."[3]

It is important to recognize that, like systemic racism broadly, environmental racism does not require overtly racist intentions.

1 United Church of Christ Commission for Racial Justice, *Toxic Wastes and Race in the United States.*

2 United Church of Christ Justice and Witness Ministries et al., *Toxic Wastes and Race at Twenty: 1987–2007,* xii.

3 United Church of Christ Justice and Witness Ministries et al., 12.

While undoubtedly some of the unequal distribution of environmental harms is due to explicitly racist decisions—someone, somewhere, choosing one site over another because of its racial demographics—environmental racism can nonetheless exist in the absence of such decisions. The existence of social and economic dynamics of inequality that push hazardous sites into Black and brown communities, even without racist intent, is systemic racism. To respond to the charge of environmental racism by saying that these dynamics are the product of economic or political forces, rather than racist motivations, is simply to shift the focus of the charge: Why are political access and economic power so unevenly distributed along racial lines that they manifest in environmental inequalities? What historical decisions have led to the current status quo, where a person's skin color directly affects the likelihood that they live in proximity to hazardous wastes? Racist redlining policies, for example, explicitly excluded families of color from certain communities, establishing the conditions for environmental inequalities that persist today. Shifting the question to inequalities of housing or income or political access does not negate the charge of racism; it simply shows how profoundly racist societal structures are. As philosopher Kristin Shrader-Frechette argues, "the issue is not whether people, corporations, or governments deliberately discriminate against poor people or minorities in siting decisions and therefore cause them to live in polluted areas ... [T]he issue is whether some citizens ought to have less than equal opportunity to breathe clean air, drink clean water, and be protected from environmental toxins."[4]

Warren County and the UCC report epitomized a confluence of streams in environmental and social thought and action in a way that would transform environmentalism, religious and secular.[5] In the environmental justice movement, the civil rights movement of

---

4 Kristin S. Shrader-Frechette, *Environmental Justice: Creating Equality, Reclaiming Democracy* (Oxford: Oxford University Press, 2002), 16.

5 Luke W. Cole and Sheila R. Foster, *From the Ground Up: Environmental Racism and the Rise of the Environmental Justice Movement*, Critical America (New York: NYU Press, 2001), 20–32.

the 1950s, 1960s, and 1970s merged with the grassroots antitoxics movement, academics studying environmental injustices, Native American activism around land, and the labor movement. Yet one significant stream remained absent. Traditional environmental organizations were long skeptical of the environmental justice movement, which they saw as too anthropocentric and political. Warren County exemplified this dynamic too. The protests pitted activists against the EPA, whose hazardous waste regulations had guided the process for disposing of the PCB-contaminated soil. These regulations were supported by the Sierra Club, which viewed the protests as political resistance to their environmental efforts and withdrew their support.[6] Even though mainstream environmental organizations like the Sierra Club had their origins in the activism and social ferment of the 1960s, alongside the civil rights and antiwar movements, with respect to environmental justice, they had progressively moved away from "justice-driven" approaches to more "conservation-driven" ones.[7] This divide manifested itself in dramatic ways, as in 1971, when a majority of Sierra Club members rejected a proposed focus on "the conservation problems of special groups such as the urban poor and ethnic minorities." It also manifested itself (and still does) in subtler ways, as in 2014, when a study of more than three hundred environmental groups in the United States found a "troubling" lack of racial diversity in the groups' leadership.[8] For decades after the emergence of the environmental justice movement, mainstream environmental organizations refused to see the whiteness inherent in their advocacy; they failed to recognize that "conserving nature always simultaneously conserves a political order."[9]

This divide within environmentalism broadly is reflected within Christian environmentalism in the United States as well, albeit in

---

6 Jenkins, *The Future of Ethics*, 202–3.

7 Jenkins, 203; Cole and Foster, *From the Ground Up*, 29.

8 Amanda J. Baugh, *God and the Green Divide: Religious Environmentalism in Black and White* (Oakland: University of California Press, 2017), 16, http://www.jstor.org/stable/10.1525/j.ctt1f89t7r.5.

9 Jenkins, *The Future of Ethics*, 203.

somewhat subtler ways; that tension is the focus of this chapter. Mainstream Christian environmentalism, to put it benignly, has been too slow to incorporate the ecological insights and lived experiences of communities of color. Some strands within that mainstream tradition have been outright resistant to those insights and experiences. To put it more pointedly, they have been racist. It is my contention here that these failures are a consequence of the whiteness inherent in the theologies of Christian environmentalism. It is a guiding claim of this book that Christian environmentalisms that are not intentionally anti-oppressive fail to reckon adequately with their own whiteness. In this chapter, I will point to four tendencies in mainstream Christian environmentalism that fall short in this regard and so reflect its whiteness: first, politics that deemphasize or universalize claims of justice; second, a worldview that privileges ostensibly apolitical science; third, an idealized view of the natural world as wilderness; and, fourth, a theology almost exclusively focused on a narrow account of creation. In subsequent chapters, I will suggest how decolonial and antiracist commitments might begin to challenge that whiteness.

These claims are broad. As discussed in Chapter 1, Christian environmentalism is internally diverse, even in what I have described as its mainstream, predominantly white, forms. Some strands within that tradition have been far more "justice-driven" and attentive to the concerns and experiences of communities of color and other marginalized groups than others, especially in recent decades. Some Christian groups have actively interrogated the racism in their past and present (like the Sierra Club began to do in 2020). And not all Christian groups are equally characterized by the tendencies I have indicated above, with respect to their conceptions of justice, science, wilderness, and creation.

Yet the testimony of environmental activists and scholars of color attests that, in general, Christian environmental groups remain unaware of the whiteness that pervades their histories and ideologies, often in subtle ways. In her study of the whiteness of worship communities, ethicist Traci West analyzes the subtle ways white privilege might be reinforced in churches' self-identification, prayers, spaces, and rituals.[10] She argues that race is always present as an issue, and denial of this reality is one of the key ways white privilege and white supremacy are perpetuated. In this chapter, I want to apply a similar lens to Christian environmentalism, drawing on West's analysis and others. First, however, we return to the environmental justice movement.

II. BEYOND ENVIRONMENTAL JUSTICE

On its face, the failure of the Sierra Club to take the Warren County protests seriously, or the similar failure of mainstream environmentalism with respect to the environmental justice movement more broadly, does not directly illustrate the whiteness of Christian environmentalism. The Sierra Club is not a Christian organization. Yet the story does bear on the themes of this chapter. The environmental justice movement, like the civil rights movement, grew out of the soil of churches, especially Black churches. Activists have emerged through church doorways, preaching sermons and singing hymns. This makes environmental justice an important site for theological creativity.[11] As they have mobilized against environmental injustices, activists have also been implicitly negotiating and renegotiating a religious cosmology and anthropology—a view of the world and of human beings as intimately connected, as ecological bodies.

This religious creativity may have put environmental justice at odds with some dominant forms of Christian environmentalism. In response to Lynn White's criticism, most approaches to religion and ecology have adopted a cosmological strategy, seeking to articulate a religious view of the world (or *cosmos*) that is ecocentric, focused on more-than-human values, rather than anthropocentric. From this

---

10 Traci C. West, *Disruptive Christian Ethics* (Louisville, KY: Westminster John Knox Press, 2006), 16–33.

11 Jenkins, *The Future of Ethics*, 206.

perspective, environmental justice may seem insufficiently theological at best—since it begins from experience and activism, rather than theological worldviews. At worst it may look narrowly anthropocentric. For some critics, environmental justice seems to be little more than NIMBY-ism (shorthand in urbanism and planning circles for "not in my back yard"—indicating opposition to new commercial and residential development within existing neighborhoods). NIMBY-ism grounds its opposition to environmental harms not in ecological awareness or group solidarity but rather in narrow self-interest. It sharpens the human-centered focus of anthropocentrism even further, to one individual or family.

This disconnect may explain why mainstream Christian environmentalism has been so slow to attend seriously to the environmental justice movement, despite its religious foundations. Yet this perspective misses the essential insights of the movement. Environmental justice does indeed begin from the human experience of ecological violence, but it then leverages that experience into a new interpretation of the world and humans' place within it.[12] Its theological method may be more problem-focused and praxis-oriented than a lot of environmental theology, but it is no less theological for that.

Even those streams of Christian environmentalism that have been attentive to justice have often failed to reckon adequately with the significance of the environmental justice movement. Recall that of the three models of Christian environmentalism discussed in Chapter 1, eco-justice is the model that has been most focused on the connections between social justice and environmental concerns.[13] Its adherents have insisted that human oppression and environmental harms are interlocking, mutually supportive pathologies, expressions of a common system of domination, and that they must be responded to accordingly. Indeed, proponents of an eco-justice model have often looked to the environmental justice movement as a crucial example

---

12 Jenkins, 205.
13 Kearns, "Saving the Creation," 57, 64.

of the needed integration of human and ecological health.[14] What this turn misses, though, are the significant differences between the two streams, particularly with respect to justice. Where eco-justice draws on a holistic conception of justice as right relations, in light of the dignity of all creation, environmental justice advocates a conception of justice that requires "distributive equity and wider political participation."[15] The latter is more directly political, more concretely aware of the complex and oppressive ways political power flows through ecological systems.[16] It demands "concrete social action," and calls for "actively questioning socioeconomic structures that exploit human and 'natural' resources."[17]

More recent work in Christian environmentalism has begun to recognize the significant theological contributions made by the environmental justice movement. Yet this recent attention may ironically further reveal the whiteness of mainstream Christian environmentalism. When environmental justice is seen as the singular Black contribution to environmentalism, the diversity of Black relationships with the natural world is reduced to a single paradigm, the experience of injustice.[18] As we will see, one way whiteness and white privilege are maintained is by reducing the experiences and insights of people of color to one type. This stereotyping may be superficially positive, as when some white Christian environmentalists turn approvingly toward environmental justice as a model; and it may

---

14 Richard R. Bohannon II and Kevin J. O'Brien, "Saving the World (and the People in It, Too): Religion in Eco-Justice and Environmental Justice," in *Inherited Land: The Changing Grounds of Religion and Ecology*, ed. Whitney A. Bauman, Richard R. Bohannon II, and Kevin J. O'Brien (Eugene, OR: Pickwick Publications, 2011), 173–76.

15 Kearns, "Religious Climate Activism in the United States," 135; Jenkins, *Ecologies of Grace*, 63.

16 I am indebted to Willis Jenkins for this phrase.

17 Karen Baker-Fletcher, *Sisters of Dust, Sisters of Spirit: Womanist Wordings on God and Creation* (Minneapolis: Fortress Press, 1998), 57.

18 Elonda Clay, "How Does It Feel to Be an Environmental Problem? Studying Religion and Ecology in the African Diaspora," in *Inherited Land: The Changing Grounds of Religion and Ecology*, ed. Whitney A. Bauman, Richard R. Bohannon II, and Kevin J. O'Brien (Eugene, OR: Pickwick Publications, 2011), 148–70.

be subtle, implicitly rather than explicitly equating environmental justice with Black religious environmentalism. Nonetheless, when Christian environmental groups look to the environmental justice movement as if it encompasses the breadth of Black experiences and knowledge of the environment, they reduce a rich and diverse history to a single characteristic, that of being "an environmental problem."[19] Moreover, this reductive view defines Black environmentalism primarily with reference to white agency, the action of racist political and economic systems and actors that perpetuate environmental injustice.

In contrast, ecowomanist author Elonda Clay points to historical practices of survival and resistance to oppression, the adaptive ecological knowledge of displaced and dispersed groups, and alternative food practices and cultures as illustrations of the breadth of Black relationships with the environment.[20] While the recognition of environmental justice as a significant ideological force is important and long overdue, taken by itself it falls far short of overcoming the whiteness of mainstream Christian environmentalism.

Of course, the rich diversity of Black experiences with the natural world is not the mainstream's only historical blind spot. Latinx and Hispanic communities and other communities of color have been heavily involved in environmental justice activism. For example, in 1988, Chemical Waste Management proposed a hazardous waste incinerator in Kettleman City, California, that would have exposed residents to PCBs and other toxic chemicals. At that time, Kettleman City was 95 percent Hispanic, with 70 percent primarily Spanish-speaking, and 40 percent exclusively Spanish-speaking. But the public hearing process was conducted only in English, and the environmental impact statement was available only in English. The residents formed a group, El Pueblo Para el Aire y Agua Limpio (The People for Clean Air and Water), that filed a lawsuit against the county, which

---

19 Clay, "How Does It Feel to Be an Environmental Problem?," 149.
20 Clay, 156–59.

had approved the incinerator, and won.[21] In this case a matter of the siting of an environmental harm laid bare problems of unequal political access.

Latinx experiences and relationships with the natural world, like Black experiences and relationships, are of course far more diverse than simply environmental justice struggles. Despite this richness, and in spite of the fact that one survey revealed Black Protestants and Hispanic Catholics to be the religious groups most concerned about climate change, these groups have habitually been excluded from mainstream environmentalism by a narrative that understands Christian environmentalism to be predominantly "a white issue."[22]

Native Americans have had an equally fraught relationship with mainstream white environmentalism.[23] Native American cultures have diverse and complex relationships to sacred spaces.[24] The trope of Native Americans as "the original environmentalists" mischaracterizes this complexity even as it underwrites perspectives and policies that continue to exploit and displace Indigenous communities.[25] Here again, Christian environmentalism is implicated. Just as Christianity endorsed the colonialist ideologies that justified the displacement and genocide of Indigenous Americans, contemporary Christianity continues to be complicit in the neocolonial erasure of Native Americans.[26] And while it may uplift certain conceptions of

---

21 "El Pueblo Para El Aire y Agua Limpio v. County of Kings," The Environmental Law Reporter, December 30, 1991, accessed August 20, 2020, https://elr.info/sites/default/files/litigation/22.20357.htm.

22 James H. Cone, "Whose Earth Is It Anyway?," *CrossCurrents* 50, no. 1/2 (April 1, 2000): 36–46; Kearns, "Ecology and Religious Environmentalism in the United States," 621.

23 Kearns, "Ecology and Religious Environmentalism in the United States," 613.

24 Vine Deloria Jr., *Spirit and Reason: The Vine Deloria, Jr. Reader*, ed. Sam Scinta and Kristen Foehner (Golden, CO: Fulcrum Publishing, 1999), 327–34.

25 Dina Gilio-Whitaker, *As Long as Grass Grows: The Indigenous Fight for Environmental Justice, from Colonization to Standing Rock*, reprint ed. (Boston: Beacon Press, 2020), 104–8.

26 Taber-Hamilton, "When Creation Is Sacred: Restoring the Indigenous Jesus," 167.

Indigenous ecological spirituality, Christian environmentalism has yet to examine fully the church's colonialist past, and to decolonize its current theologies and institutions adequately.[27]

Finally, ecofeminism has been a central discourse in Christian and religious environmentalism more broadly from the earliest stages. Ecofeminists in general contend that the same systems of patriarchy and exploitation are responsible for the oppression and degradation of the earth and of women (as well as of the poor, of people of color, of children, and of other marginalized groups). While some ecofeminists have ultimately rejected Christianity or even any religious grounding whatsoever, ecofeminist thinkers have had a profound influence on all three strands of Christian environmentalism.[28] Nonetheless, speaking from the perspective of women of color, ecowomanist writers point out that ecofeminism has reflected the same parochialism as environmentalism more broadly; that is, a predominantly white, middle-class relationship to the natural world. Ecofeminism, they argue, has been incapable of adequately incorporating the experiences of women of color.[29]

More than twenty years ago, these habitual exclusions led African American liberation theologian James Cone to ask, "Whose earth is it, anyway?" In an essay by that title, he challenges Black activists to pay more attention to the environmental movement, and environmentalists to engage in a radical critique of the white supremacy at the root of their movement.[30] In environmental ethics and theology, he says, "there is hardly a hint that perhaps whites could learn something of how we got into this ecological mess from those who have been the victims of white world supremacy."[31] He acknowledges signs of progress—white writers pointing to environmental racism,

---

27 Taber-Hamilton, 184.

28 Kearns, "Saving the Creation," 57.

29 Dorceta E. Taylor, "Women of Color, Environmental Justice, and Ecofeminism," in *Ecofeminism: Women, Culture, Nature*, ed. Karen Warren (Bloomington: Indiana University Press, 1997), 58–63.

30 Cone, "Whose Earth Is It Anyway?"

31 Cone, 42.

or including "a token black or Indian in their anthologies"—but concludes that "people of color are not treated *seriously,* as if they have something *essential* to contribute to the conversation."[32] To be sure, these positive trends have continued and increased since Cone's writing. At the same time, as the examples I have described make clear, for the most part mainstream Christian environmentalism has yet to engage in the kind of radical self-critique of its own whiteness that Cone called for over two decades ago. Such a critique requires white environmental activists and thinkers to go beyond simple inclusion to consider the whiteness that is at the very heart of much of our environmental theology. More importantly, it requires the willingness to relinquish, in truly meaningful ways, the power and privilege that whites have maintained in Christian environmentalism. I turn now to the beginnings of this kind of critique: an examination of the whiteness that is foundational to Christian environmentalism and ecotheology.

III. THE WHITENESS OF GREEN CHRISTIANITY

Why has mainstream, predominantly white environmental Christianity remained unable or unwilling to engage the kind of radical critique Cone called for more than twenty years ago? Not surprisingly, this failure is connected to similar failures in Christian theology and environmentalism more broadly. As I described in Chapter 1, the development of Christian environmentalism has overlapped with and tracked the development of secular environmentalism, adopting many of the same ideological commitments and, consequently, the same ideological blind spots. At the same time, in its theological worldview, Christian environmentalism partakes of the same strengths and shortcomings as Christian theology more broadly.

Sociologist Joe Feagin proposes the concept of "the white racial frame" as a helpful tool for understanding the subtle ways whiteness

---

32 Cone, 42 (italics in original).

pervades United States society, and I believe it is helpful in our context as well. A frame, says Feagin, is a perspectival tool, "imbedded in individual minds, as well as in collective memories and histories, [that] helps people make sense out of everyday situations."[33] In other words, it is the lens that allows us to interpret our reality in meaningful ways. In North America, a dominant frame is the white racial frame, which interprets reality in a way that tends to ascribe value to white people and their experiences, and tends to devalue the experiences of racial "others," whether in overt or subtle ways. This is not just a matter of abstract interpretation: the frame "directly shape[s] the scripts that whites and others act on," leading to discriminatory behaviors and structures.[34] Through stereotypes, prejudices, emotions, and images, the white racial frame produces concrete discrimination.

Feagin's astute analysis of the white racial frame has led environmental ethicist Christopher Carter to speak of the "white environmentalist frame," a "subframe" of the white racial frame that has shaped mainstream environmentalism according to "the ecological worldview of whiteness."[35] This frame identifies care for the environment according to a privileged, white experience of nature, with an emphasis on recreation as opposed to labor, wilderness as opposed to lived spaces, freedom as opposed to oppression, beauty as opposed to degradation and pollution, etc. The white environmental frame shapes the environmental movement, such that its well-intentioned liberal white adherents may reject aspects of the traditional white racial frame (the idea that Black people are lazy, for example), while maintaining others (the idea that Black people do not enjoy being outdoors).[36] The frame supports many of the stereotypes described in the previous section; and it accounts for the reluctance of many people of color to identify themselves with the environmental

---

33 Joe R. Feagin, *The White Racial Frame: Centuries of Racial Framing and Counter-Framing* (New York: Routledge, 2009), 10.

34 Feagin, *The White Racial Frame*, 16.

35 Carter, "Blood in the Soil," 47–48.

36 Carter, 47–48.

movement. Furthermore, Carter suggests that it is rooted in Christian theological anthropology.

In the same way that Carter examines the whiteness of environmentalism, some theologians have analyzed the whiteness that inhabits Christian theology's very foundations. In his profound and incisive book *The Christian Imagination*, theologian Willie James Jennings carefully describes how, through centuries of colonialism, Christian doctrines of creation and salvation became distorted to underwrite the concept of race and, with it, slavery and settler colonialism. As salvation became separated from God's election of Israel and instead tied to (white) European Christianity, Christian identity and election for salvation became a function of racial identity.[37] Likewise, when creation became a theological concept unconnected to any particular place, it became instead grounded in a racialized hierarchy of peoples and spaces.[38] Jennings's point is that these key theological ideas are so deeply implicated in the creation of race and colonization that decolonizing Christian theology requires fundamentally reimagining them. These theological foundations of whiteness will be the focus of Chapter 3.

As I have mentioned, ethicist Traci West shows how Christian communities, both white and those of color, might subtly reinforce white privilege in their practices. Given the insidiousness of the white racial frame, essential Christian practices can take on racialized meaning and potentially reinscribe stereotypes.[39] The universality of communion expressed in the Eucharist, for example, can be taken as a denial of cultural specificity and sociopolitical inequalities. A eucharistic theology of substitutionary atonement might serve, she suggests, to support a sense of entitled privilege. Prayers for and outreach toward impoverished or disadvantaged groups can reinforce a sense of distance and superiority. Even impulses toward inclusivity or multiculturalism can paradoxically perpetuate the whiteness

---

37 Willie James Jennings, *The Christian Imagination: Theology and the Origins of Race* (New Haven, CT: Yale University Press, 2011), 32–33.

38 Jennings, *The Christian Imagination*, 58.

39 West, *Disruptive Christian Ethics*, 124–25.

they seek to disrupt, if they fail to examine critically structures of privilege and white supremacy.[40] This is the sort of denial that West says is fundamental to maintaining white privilege; and it is why decolonial and antiracist analyses are so critical.

Mainstream environmentalism and Christian theology both incorporate foundational ideas that produce and reinforce racial discrimination, as these authors demonstrate. In their own ways, they participate in and perpetuate the white racial frame. Put bluntly, they incorporate racist assumptions. Since Christian environmentalism emerges from these two roots, it stands to reason that it incorporates its own racial assumptions that need to be interrogated. In what follows, I address four such assumptions: a conception of justice that is either weak or overly general; a view of science as apolitical; a focus on the natural world as wilderness; and a reliance on a narrow account of creation. These assumptions constitute the whiteness of green Christianity.

1. The Reach of Justice

Justice has not been central to some forms of Christian environmentalism. Using the broad categories described in Chapter 1, neither the concept of justice nor accounts of environmental injustices figure prominently in the Stewardship or Creation Spirituality models. These approaches have been "more oriented toward recovering God in the creation than in realizing the kingdom of God on earth; more concerned with preaching the implications of science than those of economic and social injustice."[41] Arguably the dominant creation care ethic in North America has been primarily focused on more-than-human nature, with little attention to human social and economic issues: an ecocentric—some would say misanthropic—ethic.[42] This

---

40 West, 134–38.
41 Kearns, "Saving the Creation," 57–58.
42 Raymond E. Grizzle and Christopher B. Barrett, "The One Body of Christian Environmentalism," *Zygon* 33, no. 2 (June 1, 1998): 239–40; Shrader-Frechette, *Environmental Justice*, 4.

is surely an understandable focus, and it is at least partly a reaction to Lynn White's charge that Christianity is fundamentally and perniciously anthropocentric.

Yet many Christian environmental thinkers, including environmental justice advocates and scholars and activists of color, argue that this focus is mistaken. Some, like ecofeminists and ecowomanists, insist that the two pathologies—environmental degradation and human oppression—are mutually reinforcing, and to view them as separate or even competitive concerns only makes things worse. Others, like Cone, argue that it is racist for "white people [to] care more about the endangered whale and the spotted owl than they do about the survival of young blacks in our nation's cities."[43]

The exception to this divide (aside from environmental justice) has, again, been the eco-justice approach. Early in the development of the environmental movement, a significant contingent of Christian denominations articulated a focus on eco-justice, expanding a concern for social justice to include the environment and justice's ecological aspects. In 1983 the National Council of Churches, representing primarily Protestant denominations but also Eastern Orthodox churches, formed the Eco-Justice Working Group to develop these themes.[44] The group paid particular attention to the environmental justice movement from the beginning. The National Council of Churches published its own report on environmental racism in 1986, as well as a formal declaration that explicitly tied together the terms eco-justice and environmental justice. The neglect of justice in other branches of Christian environmentalism was not the case with eco-justice.

Yet as I have noted, two fundamentally different conceptions of justice are operative here. One is general and holistic, the other concrete and radical. Eco-justice's religious affirmation of justice in terms of restored relationships is not the same as environmental justice's political demand for recognition and equity. Even when the

---

43 Cone, "Whose Earth Is It Anyway?," 36–37.
44 Kearns, "Ecology and Religious Environmentalism in the United States," 610.

Eco-Justice Working Group sought to link the two terms, they arguably misrepresented environmental justice: "Environmental Justice
is a holistic term that includes all ministries designed to heal and
defend creation. Eco-justice is an even broader term that includes
efforts to assure justice for all of creation and the human beings
who live in it."[45] While these definitions correctly name the greater
breadth of eco-justice, they do not accurately portray the concrete
and political character of environmental justice.

The primary conceptions of justice in mainstream Christian environmentalism have been either too weak or too general to reckon
with the claims of environmental racism and injustice. They have not
supported the kind of antiracist and decolonial work that is needed to
examine and challenge white privilege within the movement. Instead,
they have perpetuated the whiteness of Christian environmentalism.
An overly universalized understanding of justice, as in eco-justice, fails
to see how environmental injustices do not affect all people equally.

One clear example of this is the inability to reckon adequately
with the oppressive history of humans' relationship to the earth.
Mainstream accounts of alienation from the natural world have,
until recently, rarely included descriptions of those whose historical
relationship to the land included forced displacement (as for Native
Americans) or forced emplacement (as for slaves and their descendants). As environmental ethicist Larry Rasmussen puts it, "the
history of coercion, brutality, cultural genocide, and worse is not part
of the moral memory and narrative of most environmental organizations. . . . In stark contrast, this history and these peoples are always
part of the memory of the [environmental justice] movement, and
the reason it channels rage that is centuries deep. The moral worlds
of [environmental justice] and other environmentalists differ mark-
edly from one another."[46]

---

45 Kearns, 611; cf. Larry Rasmussen, "Environmental Racism and Environmental Justice: Moral Theory in the Making?," *Journal of the Society of Christian
Ethics* 24, no. 1 (2004): 3–28.

46 Rasmussen, "Environmental Racism and Environmental Justice: Moral
Theory in the Making?," 10.

A related shortcoming in Christian environmentalism has been a tendency to focus on personal responsibility, rather than systemic political and economic transformation. For stewardship and creation spirituality approaches, individual conversion is seen as a primary orientation. An eco-justice approach attends more explicitly to the political and economic forces that drive environmental crises.[47] Nonetheless, in practice, mainstream Christian environmentalism has typically focused more on the actions of individuals and congregations—recycling, reducing single-use disposable items, so-called "greening the church" projects—rather than advocating for systemic change. This, of course, is not accidental, nor is it entirely churches' fault. Polluting corporations like fossil fuel producers and beverage and packaging companies invest massive resources in perpetuating consumers' sense of responsibility and downplaying the need for major systemic transformations.

2. The Role of Science

If Christian environmentalism's account of justice has been insufficiently political, its view of the role of science has been even less so. This may seem uncontroversial—of course an environmental movement would rely on science, and of course science would be politically neutral. Such a view is too sanguine: as with justice, uncritical appeals to science do not serve all people equally.

The main approach of many Christian environmentalists has been to view the natural sciences as an unproblematic ally.[48] For these environmentalists, the insights of the sciences can provide both clear evidence of the imminent crises and the necessary solutions, while for its part religious faith can provide motivation and perhaps some spiritual overlays to the sciences' hard data. Ecology, which emerged as a field in the late nineteenth century but surged alongside

---

47 Kearns, "Saving the Creation," 56.
48 Kearns, 57–58.

the environmental movement, has seemed an especially promising partner for religious environmentalists. Ecology approaches species, habitats, and their interactions holistically, seeking to understand the relationships and connections among them. For religious thinkers, this makes ecology an ideal shorthand for interconnectedness— supporting not just descriptions of complex systems but normative moral and theological appeals to a sense of harmony and even communion.[49] These sorts of appeals mischaracterize the complexity and analytical value of ecology as a science. Ecology doesn't simply demonstrate that species and systems are connected; rather, it begins from that interconnectedness and examines the nature of those relationships in order to understand, predict, and intervene in those systems.

Perhaps more significantly, such a rosy conception of ecology may also narrow the scope of religious environmentalism in ways that contribute to its whiteness. Normative appeals to harmony can shift focus exclusively toward places and ecosystems that seem to be balanced and harmonious. This can reinforce an image of pristine wilderness and take attention away from anything that contradicts that image, such as degraded ecosystems or destructive or predatory relationships among species. This one-sided view may therefore have difficulty thinking theologically about working environments and what some have called "environmental sacrifice zones," places that disproportionately bear the environmental costs of our society. Yet such places are often precisely those that shape the ecological experiences of many marginalized communities.

Here, too, the environmental justice movement challenges the idea that science is always a neutral ally. In environmental justice battles like Warren County, official scientific research has often been mobilized in service of dominant parties, like the government and corporations.

---

49 Sarah Fredericks and Kevin J. O'Brien, "The Importance and Limits of Taking Science Seriously: Data and Uncertainty in Religion and Ecology," in *Inherited Land: The Changing Grounds of Religion and Ecology*, ed. Whitney A. Bauman, Richard R. Bohannon II, and Kevin J. O'Brien (Eugene, OR: Pickwick Publications, 2011), 45–46.

Research on the effects or potential effects of the siting of environmental harms can function to undermine efforts for environmental justice through overt or subtle means, by choosing what parameters to follow and what data to exclude. For example, Environmental Impact Statements, which are used to make decisions about potentially harmful projects, may describe potential benefits in quantitative terms but potential harms in qualitative terms, making the latter easier to discount.[50]

The 2007 UCC report extensively documents the story of the Holt family of Dickson, Tennessee.[51] A county landfill was established near the predominantly Black community of Eno Road in Dickson, fifty-four feet from the farm of the Holt family, a Black family with deep roots in the community. Beginning in 1988, tests by government agencies showed the presence of the chemical trichloroethylene (TCE) in the Holts' well water in excess of the established maximum contaminant level (MCL), the maximum amount of a contaminant allowed in drinking water by the Environmental Protection Agency (EPA). But because some tests showed lower levels, the high levels were dismissed as testing errors, and the Holts were repeatedly told that their well water was safe. Then, for nine years, as the government periodically tested private wells within a one-mile radius of the landfill, the Holts' well was never retested. When the well was finally tested twice in 2000, TCE levels were found to be twenty-four and twenty-nine times the MCL set by the EPA. The family was notified and was put on county water. The water was first provided at the county's expense, but the county stopped paying for it after the family filed a lawsuit against the city and the county. While the county commission voted unanimously to settle lawsuits with several white families in the region whose wells were contaminated, as of the writing of the report, they had not settled with the Holts. Moreover, when the wells of nine white families near an automotive manufacturing plant in Dickson were found to be contaminated with TCE, they were notified within

---

50 Shrader-Frechette, *Environmental Justice*, 43.

51 United Church of Christ Justice and Witness Ministries et al., *Toxic Wastes and Race at Twenty*, 137–48.

forty-eight hours, given bottled water, and placed on the city water system. It had taken twelve years from the initial positive test for the Holts to receive even a remotely comparable response.[52]

The story of the Holt family indicates a number of systemic failures, such the failure of the regulatory system, unequal application of environmental protections, and a lack of access to the political system. It also demonstrates how even the hard data of science can be manipulated or misused by those with power. The dismissal of critical tests as outliers and the failure to test the Holts' well for nine years were decisions with political and ecological implications. And this kind of inequality is systemic: studies have shown that assessments of health risks of toxic sites consistently underestimate those risks, regularly failing to meet the government-established safety benchmarks.[53] In one study, assessments for four sites failed to meet a total of thirty-nine out of forty government-mandated requirements for adequate sampling.

On a larger scale, we can note the ways scientists, as human beings, are inevitably subject to biases, especially when their research is funded by industries that stand to gain from it. A particularly well-known example of this is, of course, studies sponsored by fossil fuel companies that downplayed the reality of climate change.[54] In fact, the companies used some of the same researchers that had cast doubt on the dangers of tobacco to promote similar ambiguities around climate change and air pollution.[55] The question of who controls scientific

---

52 United Church of Christ Justice and Witness Ministries et al., *Toxic Wastes and Race at Twenty*, 143.

53 Kristin Shrader-Frechette and Andrew M. Biondo, "Health Misinformation about Toxic-Site Harm: The Case for Independent-Party Testing to Confirm Safety," *International Journal of Environmental Research and Public Health* 18, no. 3882 (April 1, 2021): https://doi.org/10.3390/ijerph18083882; Kristin Shrader-Frechette and Andrew M. Biondo, "Data-Quality Assessment Signals Toxic-Site Safety Threats and Environmental Injustices," *International Journal of Environmental Research and Public Health* 18, no. 2012 (February 1, 2021): https://doi.org/10.3390/ijerph18042012.

54 Fredericks and O'Brien, "The Importance and Limits of Taking Science Seriously," 52.

55 Benjamin Hulac, "Tobacco and Oil Industries Used Same Researchers to Sway Public," *Scientific American*, July 20, 2016, accessed

knowledge, and controls access to that knowledge, is a political matter, and a matter of justice. Science is not politically neutral.

Indigenous voices have been among the most astute critics of how science can be and has been used to serve political ends. Standing Rock Sioux theologian Vine Deloria Jr. points to the scientific method itself, which he argues is too restricted when compared with the holism of supposedly "prescientific" Native worldviews: "Western science has drawn its conclusions by excluding the kinds of data that the Western Sioux cherished. . . . Thus most emotional experiences of human beings are discarded as unsuitable for the scientific enterprise."[56] He draws on historian Thomas Kuhn's influential work on paradigms in science, which demonstrates just how thoroughly scientific inquiry is shaped by convention. By contrast, Native American knowledge, Deloria argues, is as rigorous and systematic as Western science, but also more comprehensive in its scope, and indeed more sophisticated.[57] Historically, the subjugation of this knowledge in the name of a worldview that was both scientific and supposedly Christian provided ideological support for the forced removal of Native Americans from their lands.[58]

But this subjugation of Indigenous knowledge in the name of scientific rigor is not only a historical phenomenon. In her stunning book *Braiding Sweetgrass,* biologist and member of the Citizen Potawatomi Tribe Robin Wall Kimmerer describes her own experience of having to suppress the questions and insights of her heritage for the sake of scientific objectivity.[59] She recounts how the beauty of asters and goldenrod growing side by side led her to inquire into the "architecture of relationships," and how this inquiry was stifled

---

May 25, 2022, https://www.scientificamerican.com/article/tobacco-and-oil-industries-used-same-researchers-to-sway-public1/.

56 Deloria, *Spirit and Reason*, 44.

57 Deloria, 67.

58 Deloria, 202–3.

59 Robin Wall Kimmerer, *Braiding Sweetgrass: Indigenous Wisdom, Scientific Knowledge and the Teachings of Plants* (Minneapolis: Milkweed Editions, 2015), 39–47.

by established scientists. She points out, too, that this suppression of intimate knowledge of and relationship to land was, even in the twentieth century, a means to the expropriation of Native peoples.[60]

Scientific knowledge of ecosystems, gleaned from ecology, climatology, biology, or other natural sciences, is essential to environmental health and human health, as is knowledge from the social sciences and humanities. What is problematic, however, is the straightforward assumption that science is, or can be, value neutral or apolitical. In both the past and the present, scientific research is shaped by politics and culture; its questions and paradigms reflect unequal power dynamics. "Because ecologies are political," says Willis Jenkins, "ecological knowledge unavoidably shapes and serves political ends."[61] Christian environmentalism should not dismiss the value of scientific research. If it wishes to overcome its whiteness, however, it will need to be critical of science's limitations and blind spots.

3. The Image of Wilderness

Just as mainstream Christian environmentalism inherits a reliance on science from secular environmentalism, it also inherits a fraught relationship with the notion of wilderness. Indeed, in some ways, the North American fascination with wilderness has its roots in Christianity and Judaism, where it has had various meanings. The Hebrew Bible, and to a lesser extent, the New Testament, demonstrates this polyvalence: wilderness can be a place of danger or trial, as in the Exodus from Egypt; a place of refuge, as it was for Hagar; or a place of spiritual retreat or encounter (which does not exclude danger, of course), as for Moses and Jesus.[62]

---

60 Kimmerer, *Braiding Sweetgrass*, 16–19.
61 Jenkins, *The Future of Ethics*, 218.
62 Roderick Frazier Nash, *Wilderness and the American Mind*, 5th ed. (New Haven, CT: Yale University Press, 2014), 13–17.

Yet the idea of wilderness took on a new salience when Europeans began colonizing North America in the sixteenth century.[63] Fear of the wilderness and its "savage" inhabitants combined with the desire for economic prosperity and Christian theology to forge a powerful imagination of wilderness in the minds of colonists. With a few exceptions, the attitude of European colonists associated wilderness with physical and spiritual danger, and perceived a distinctive call to subjugate the untamed land.

When, in the nineteenth and twentieth centuries, Romanticism led to a shift in attitudes toward a more positive assessment of wilderness, and particularly of its spiritual value, it nonetheless left many of the main characteristics of wilderness—as "solitary, mysterious, and chaotic"—intact.[64] For patriarchs of the modern environmental movement like Henry David Thoreau and John Muir, wilderness maintained some of the awesome numinous power their colonial forbears had perceived; yet this power was now understood as salutary and even beneficent.

This is the broad imagination of wilderness inherited by twentieth-century environmentalists: pristine and natural, powerful and tinged with sacredness, above all a contrast (whether threatening or edifying) to settled agricultural or urban lands. More contemporary versions nuance these earlier conceptions, especially by shifting the emphasis from how wilderness serves human physical and spiritual needs to its own intrinsic value as a source of biodiversity. Nonetheless, the importance of wilderness for environmentalism, with its religious and sometimes specifically Christian resonances, has remained significant.[65] This centrality is reflected, among other

---

63 Bron Taylor, "Wilderness, Spirituality and Biodiversity in North America—Tracing an Environmental History from Occidental Roots to Earth Day," in *Wilderness in Mythology and Religion: Approaching Religious Spatialities, Cosmologies, and Ideas of Wild Nature*, ed. Laura Feldt (Boston: De Gruyter, 2012), 297–98, https://doi.org/10.1515/9781614511724.293.

64 Nash, *Wilderness and the American Mind*, 44.

65 Taylor, "Wilderness, Spirituality and Biodiversity in North America," 318–19.

places, in the establishment of the National Parks, the Wilderness Act of 1964, and the Endangered Species Act of 1973.

For all the concrete good it has engendered, there are problems with this common imagination of wilderness. The contrast with settled agricultural and urban lands, for example, illustrates a troubling dualism that separates humans from the more-than-human world. Like the oversimplified ecological harmony described in the previous section, this can lead to a narrow focus on supposedly natural spaces, and a neglect of inhabited places, working landscapes, and degraded spaces.

This relates to an elitism that many see in the wilderness ideal. Whether by explicit policy or unwritten social norm, access to wilderness spaces is often the purview of an elite few (in North America, mainly relatively affluent whites). This elitism, in turn, reflects the problematic history of wilderness. The production first of the idea of wilderness, then of wilderness spaces themselves, required the erasure of those who inhabited and used the land. The notion of an untrammeled wilderness, untouched by human impact, has always ignored the skillful and careful ways Indigenous communities managed their habitats. Then, motivated by these illusions, National Parks and other so-called wild spaces were created by forcibly removing or excluding those communities from these supposedly pristine places. Muir explicitly used the wilderness idea as justification for the coercive enforcement of this unjust sense of purity.

Again, Christian theology has been directly implicated in these imaginations from the start. The early colonial imagination of wilderness (and its Indigenous inhabitants) as a threat in need of transformation is deeply rooted in a Christian theology of salvation, or soteriology. The encounter with a new world necessitated a radically new theology, and colonial Christianity responded with a soteriology that divided people and places into a hierarchy of salvation, with whiteness as the defining characteristic.[66] Nonwhite peoples were closely associated with their wild lands, and both were equally in

---

66 Jennings, *The Christian Imagination.*

need of transformation by Christian colonizers. Similarly, a Christian interpretation of the Genesis creation account as *creatio ex nihilo*, or creation out of nothing, contributed to the lie that the new world was *terra nullius*, an empty land available for the taking.[67] The logic of *creatio ex nihilo*, where God is understood to create from nothing (as opposed to creating out of "the deep," the primordial chaos of Genesis 1:2), was transferred to (white European) human beings, who could reproduce God's image by dominating and cultivating the "nothing" of supposedly untouched wild nature. This logic erases both the value of the natural world itself and the prior agency of Indigenous peoples on and with it.

Mainstream Christian environmentalism, like environmentalism broadly, has nuanced its understanding of wilderness to recognize some of these problematic aspects. The basic ideological and theological architecture, however, persists: the idea that wilderness is a place set apart, over against lived and degraded spaces. By contrast, environmental justice groups and other critics of this view tend to see human and environmental needs as mutually dependent. They tend to focus not on wilderness spaces or places of recreation but rather on working landscapes, lived spaces, and places of environmental injustice.[68] Thus the theological and ideological orientation toward wilderness contributes to the whiteness of Christian environmentalism.

4. The Theology of Creation

At least since Lynn White's influential indictment of Christianity, Christian environmentalists have felt compelled to ground their

---

67 Whitney A. Bauman, "Creatio Ex Nihilo, Terra Nullius, and the Erasure of Presence," in *Ecospirit: Religions and Philosophies for the Earth*, ed. Laurel Kearns and Catherine Keller, Transdisciplinary Theological Colloquia (New York: Fordham University Press, 2007), 353–72.

68 Taylor, "Women of Color, Environmental Justice, and Ecofeminism," 54–55.

environmental theology in the creation accounts of Genesis. From Bible studies and creation care committee meetings to magisterial statements like Pope Francis's *Laudato Si'*, Christian environmental reflection inevitably devotes significant theological attention to the first chapters of Genesis. In more extended studies, other texts of the Old Testament (and, to an even lesser extent, the New Testament) may receive some consideration. But for many Christians, environmental theology begins—and typically ends—with the first chapters of the Bible. To offer one anecdotal example: a doctoral-level course I co-teach on biblical understandings of land intentionally begins with selections from Deuteronomy and Leviticus related to the how the Israelites are to relate to their promised land, such as Sabbath and Jubilee laws, and with the food-policy narrative of Joseph in Pharaoh's service, rather than with the creation accounts. My co-instructor and I point this out and explain the reasons for this choice. Nonetheless, invariably most of the projects submitted for the course deal almost exclusively with the Genesis creation accounts.

Like the embrace of science and wilderness, this focus seems natural and unproblematic: Where else would Christians turn for the foundations of environmental theology? Yet the Genesis accounts—which, it always bears repeating, are not one unified account but represent at least two distinct stories—are not the only creation stories in the Christian Bible, or even the oldest ones. They are simply the first in canonical order. Proverbs recounts the role of personified Wisdom in the creation of the world (Prov 8). A similar role is ascribed to God's word in Psalm 33, which is associated with Jesus in the creation account found in the preface to the Gospel of John (John 1:1-4). Other psalms recount their own creation narratives (Pss 8, 89, and 104, to name a few). Job contains multiple accounts of the creation (e.g., Job 26, 28, 38). And the book of Revelation gives an account of the new creation, with striking ecological imagery (e.g., Rev 22). Of course, these are just accounts of the event of creation; there are countless other texts with ecological implications, such as the ones with which my colleague and I begin our course.

Why does this matter? The Genesis accounts, especially when treated as a single unified account that centers on a garden, establishes certain themes for humans' relationship to creation. I have already described how one interpretation, the doctrine of *creatio ex nihilo*, has supported colonization and genocide. But leaving aside that particular reading, in general the Genesis stories present an orderly creation, a harmonious whole, with individual humans as the centerpiece of creation. What is crucially missing from these texts is any human society. The only relationships are between humans, God, and the land and animals, and between the man and woman (of course, interpretations of the Genesis account of this latter relationship, between the genders, have been incredibly fraught, to say the least; unfortunately, there is not space to attend to this set of difficulties here). These themes reinforce some of the problematic ideologies already mentioned: dualism between humans and creation, an illusory and narrow sense of harmony, the false belief that right relationship with creation does not necessarily demand justice for our fellow human beings, and potentially even the erasure of other human beings from supposedly pristine spaces. They also perpetuate the idea, described above, that care of creation is primarily about personal responsibility, rather than systemic transformation.

The Genesis accounts are essential to a robust environmental theology, and there are environmentally sensitive interpretations of these texts that draw out their sophisticated ecological worldview—for example, by exploring the subtleties of "dominion" and "conquering" in 1:28, or "till and keep" in 2:15.[69] I am not suggesting that these texts, or the themes they present, are not of great value for Christian environmentalism. Rather, the problem is too narrow a focus on these texts (and often without such careful exegesis), which lends itself to a relatively one-sided perspective.

Foregrounding other creation texts, in addition to the Genesis accounts, might give a more multivocal view. Where the story in

---

69 Ellen F. Davis, *Scripture, Culture, and Agriculture: An Agrarian Reading of the Bible* (New York: Cambridge University Press, 2009), 29–32, 53–63.

Genesis 2 seems to communicate the centrality of humankind, the various accounts in Job clearly portray our insignificance. The story of the exodus from Egypt, the conquest of Canaan, and Levitical laws about land use convey a complex reality where social relations and relationships with the land intersect, at times leading to prosperity and mutuality, at others to exploitation and exclusion. These texts, like the story of Joseph mentioned above, point to the land as a political reality; that is, a biblical relationship with the land is a matter of how relationships within society are organized. Doing justice for one another and for the land requires rightly ordered relationships, with one another and with God. Finally, Revelation mobilizes an account of the creation of a new heaven and new earth as a challenge to the imperial power of Rome—a boldly political theology of creation. The potential of these and other theological themes for a decolonial and antiracist Christian environmentalism will be explored in Chapter 4.

Beyond the question of which creation accounts are used, however, is a crucial question of how Christians read creation. According to Willie Jennings, the colonial imagination that transforms the land into a commodity and transforms nonwhite peoples into racialized Others begins with supersessionism, the "idea that Christians and the church have replaced Israel as the chosen people of God."[70] Supersessionism inverts the covenant theology of the Old Testament, identifying the church as God's elect, and identifying the Jews as those outside God's election. In relation to a doctrine of creation, supersessionism contends that because Christians recognize Jesus as God, they are the first to recognize God rightly as creator—forgetting that Christians inherit their accounts of creation from the Hebrew scriptures.[71] Or, as Jennings puts it, Christians position themselves as "first readers" of both the world and of Scripture, as if we were the first to encounter God there; and Jews are moved to the position of second readers.

---

70 Willie James Jennings, "Reframing the World: Toward an Actual Christian Doctrine of Creation," *International Journal of Systematic Theology* 21, no. 4 (October 1, 2019): 388–407, https://doi.org/10.1111/ijst.12385.

71 Jennings, "Reframing the World," 393.

Most theologies of creation, according to Jennings, are supersessionist in this way, in that "they would exist completely intact if there was no people called Israel at all and no mention of an Israel in the Christian scriptures."[72] This erasure of an entire people and their history is directly related to the aforementioned erasure of Native Americans and their people: by imagining themselves as first readers, Christians assume that particular histories of particular people in particular places are unimportant. Creation, as a concept, becomes fungible, transferable. This gives way to the commodification and racialization of colonialism: since colonialist Christians assumed they knew God the creator more directly, more rightly, than the peoples they displaced, both land and peoples could be subjugated to their ends.

The alternative, Jennings urges, is to become second readers again. Second readers acknowledge that they are entering the stories of another people, attending to and learning about God from the ways of other creatures. It is, he says, a "pedagogy of joining."[73] We will consider what this attitude of second readership might require of Christian environmentalism in Chapters 4 and 5. At this point, however, it is important simply to recognize that the whiteness of mainstream Christian environmentalism is related to its reading of creation stories, including which stories it focuses on and how it reads them. A narrow reading of the Genesis creation stories from an imagined position as first readers neglects a wide range of contrasting accounts, and is complicit in the erasure of non-Christian and nonwhite peoples.

IV. CONCLUSION

Green Christianity is white. By this I mean that in some of its fundamental assumptions, Christian environmentalism incorporates

---

72 Jennings, 393.
73 Jennings, 394.

aspects of an ecological worldview that is characteristically white (and relatively affluent). It emerges from historical soil that has often been overtly racist and colonialist. Contemporary Christian environmentalism has made significant efforts to overcome this history, and many of these groups and denominations have made admirable strides in decolonizing and deracializing their theologies and ideologies. Yet many central theological and ecological themes, such as those I have described here, remain characterized by whiteness. To be more specific, mainstream Christian environmentalism remains white insofar as it incorporates a notion of justice that is universal rather than partisan and participatory, uncritically relies on the natural sciences as if they were politically neutral, focuses primarily on imagined wilderness spaces to the exclusion of lived, worked, and degraded spaces, and builds its theologies on the first chapters of Genesis, often read in a way that erases the story of Israel. The problem, however, runs deeper than any of these traits.

As James Cone charged over twenty years ago, environmental theology (and we can extend the charge to mainstream Christian environmentalism more broadly) has been too slow to attend adequately to the perspectives of people of color. Even (perhaps especially) when white theologians and activists look to the environmental justice movement as a paradigmatic example of Christian environmental concern, scholars and activists of color contend that the breadth and import of their experiences of the natural world are not being fully heeded. They resist being reduced to an environmental problem, as Elonda Clay puts it.[74]

This is a practical problem, as environmental groups of all sorts lament the lack of diversity in their leadership and membership. If those groups, including Christian environmental groups, are perceived to represent a primarily white experience of the natural world, they will continue to struggle to increase their diversity. More problematically, though, they will fail to see and support the urgent and dynamic work being done by those organizations, typically

---

74 Clay, "How Does It Feel to Be an Environmental Problem?"

outside what I have characterized as the mainstream, who do incorporate broader worldviews and mandates.

It is also, more fundamentally, a theological problem, as I will show more fully in the next chapter. Colonialism, racism, and supersessionism distort the Gospel. They represent a "broken theological anthropology."[75] Christian environmentalism's invocations of wholeness and community ring false as long as they are underwritten by theological whiteness.

What will it take, then, to make mainstream Christian environmentalism less white, to deconstruct the white environmentalist frame, and transform our ecotheology to one of joining? The next chapters will turn to decolonial and antiracist theologies in order to venture a response to this challenge.

---

75 Carter, "Blood in the Soil," 46.

CHAPTER 3

The Idolatry of Whiteness and Knowledge in the Gaps

In Anaheim, California, in 2009, the 76th General Convention of the Episcopal Church formally repudiated the doctrine of discovery "as fundamentally opposed to the Gospel of Jesus Christ and our understanding of the inherent rights that individuals and peoples have received from God." The resolution pointed out that the doctrine "continues to be invoked, in only slightly modified form, in court cases and in the many destructive policies of governments and other institutions of the modern nation-state that lead to the colonizing dispossession of the lands of indigenous peoples and the disruption of their way of life." It called on the church to review its policies and programs with the goal of eliminating the ongoing influence of the doctrine of discovery, and even to write to Queen Elizabeth II, as the head of its counterpart, the Church of England, to request that she also repudiate the doctrine.[1] Other churches followed suit, including the Unitarian Universalist Association, the United Methodist Church, various yearly meetings of the Society of

---

1 "Acts of Convention: Resolution # 2009-D035," accessed September 22, 2021, https://www.episcopalarchives.org/cgi-bin/acts/acts_resolution.pl?resolution=2009-D035.

Friends (Quakers), and the World Council of Churches.[2] As of this writing, twenty-one church bodies were listed as having formally repudiated the doctrine.[3] On various occasions, Indigenous groups have written to and met with the pope to request that he formally rescind the papal bulls that established the doctrine, but he has so far declined to do so.[4]

In its responses, the Roman Catholic Church has suggested that the bulls in question represent "a historic remnant" with no moral or doctrinal value.[5] To the contrary, argue Mark Charles and Soong-Chan Rah, "the Doctrine of Discovery, rooted in fifteenth-century theological dysfunction, is one of the most influential yet hidden narratives in American society that continues to impact social reality in American society well into the twenty-first century."[6]

In this chapter, I will take the doctrine of discovery as emblematic of the theological problem of whiteness. The previous chapter demonstrated the whiteness of green Christianity—that is, the characteristics of mainstream Christian environmentalism that operate out of a distinctively white, privileged perspective, and continue to perpetuate that perspective, despite efforts to be more inclusive and racially sensitive. I pointed to four specific characteristics that reflect

---

2 Vinnie Rotondaro, "Doctrine of Discovery: A Scandal in Plain Sight," *National Catholic Reporter*, September 5, 2015, https://www.ncronline.org/news/justice/doctrine-discovery-scandal-plain-sight.

3 Indigenous Values Initiative, "Repudiations by Faith Communities," Doctrine of Discovery, July 30, 2018, https://doctrineofdiscovery.org/faith-communities/.

4 Mary Ann McGivern, "Indian Nations Ask Pope Francis to Rescind Doctrine of Discovery," *National Catholic Reporter*, December 28, 2018, https://www.ncronline.org/news/opinion/ncr-today/indian-nations-ask-pope-francis-rescind-doctrine-discovery.

5 The Long March to Rome, "The Creator Has Been Heard," accessed September 22, 2021, http://longmarchtorome.com/the-creator-has-been-heard/.

6 Mark Charles and Soong-Chan Rah, *Unsettling Truths: The Ongoing, Dehumanizing Legacy of the Doctrine of Discovery*, illustrated ed. (Downers Grove, IL: IVP Books, 2019), 38. Charles and Rah capitalize "Doctrine of Discovery." I choose not to, since the ideas it refers to are never formally articulated as a doctrine.

this whiteness. The problem, however, lies deeper than any particular set of characteristics. Whiteness emerges out of contaminated theological soil; rather than simply being misplaced emphasis or a too-narrow focus, it represents a deeply distorted theology. More than just a problem *for* theology, it is a problem *of* theology. Challenging the whiteness of Christian environmentalism will require more than broadening the scope of environmental problems or increasing the diversity of environmental leadership, though it will require those things. As this chapter will show, an anti-oppressive Christian environmentalism will have to go beyond these steps to a radical assessment of how we think theologically.

Accordingly, rather than focusing on ecotheology, in general this chapter will be more broadly theological, addressing theological themes like creation and salvation. At times I will point out implications for ecotheology. And the next two chapters will bring the theological ideas considered here back to ecotheology and Christian environmentalism specifically, to show how these ideas might transform our environmental worldviews and practices.

This project is daunting. It requires both deconstructing some of our existing ways of thinking and laying a path for new ways. This chapter will address both tasks. The insights of decoloniality are helpful for the first task. Recall from Chapter 1 that decoloniality is a group of arguments that show how power and knowledge are used to continue systems of coloniality that are part of modernity. Decoloniality originally emerged in Latin America, as resistance to the dominance of colonial ways of knowing in that context. Because those ways of knowing are so central to the systems of colonialism and racism that have developed in North America, as we will see, decolonial critiques clarify what is needed to undermine their dominance in this context. Specifically, decoloniality points to the need for more ambiguous, pluralist ways of knowing—what I will describe as ways of knowing "in the gaps."

With respect to the second task, that of beginning to lay a new path, we can begin to name what this knowing in the gaps might require. Before turning, in the next chapter, to some particular theological themes for an anti-oppressive Christian environmentalism, then, it will be helpful to think about method—that is, about how we ought to do ecotheology, what we are doing when we do ecotheology, and what we might expect from an anti-oppressive ecotheology. At the end of this chapter, then, I will identify some key characteristics of what an ecotheology in the gaps involves.

As we saw in Chapter 1, decolonization must be more than just ideological; it cannot be reduced to a metaphor. Likewise, the doctrine of discovery is a legal and political framework with real material consequences. To dismantle the legacy the doctrine represents requires concrete, material changes, such as reparations and land restitution (that is, giving the land back). By approaching whiteness and colonialism as a theological problem in this chapter, I am not suggesting that confronting it on that level is sufficient, and in Chapter 5, I will address those concrete steps toward dismantling whiteness. But whiteness is also a theological problem—indeed, it is idolatrous—and this chapter confronts that aspect of it.

I. THE DOCTRINE OF DISCOVERY

The doctrine of discovery is a legal and theological framework that has been used from the fifteenth century until the twenty-first century to justify the expropriation of land and the oppression, exploitation, and genocide of Black and brown bodies.[7] The doctrine originates in a series of papal bulls written in the fifteenth century. The first of these, *Dum Diversas*, was issued by Nicholas V in 1452. *Dum Diversas* granted King Alfonso V of Portugal papal permission

> to invade, search out, capture, vanquish, and subdue all Saracens [Muslims] and pagans whatsoever, and other enemies of Christ where-soever placed, and the kingdoms, dukedoms, principalities, domin-ions, possessions, and all movable and immovable goods whatsoever

---

7 Charles and Rah, *Unsettling Truths*.

held and possessed by them and to reduce their persons to perpetual slavery.[8]

Pope Nicholas reaffirmed the right of King Alfonso and Prince Henry of Portugal to possess non-Christian lands and enslave non-Christian peoples in a subsequent bull, *Romanus Pontifex*, in 1454. The geographic focus of these bulls was the lands of North and West Africa, and the bulls would provide explicit justification for the establishment of the African slave trade, in which Henry was a key agent.

A later bull written by Alexander VI in 1493, *Inter Caetera*, extended this papal permission to Spain's claims in the Americas. In *Inter Caetera*, Alexander praised Christopher Columbus and affirmed him as the discoverer of the Americas and an instrument of God's will to bring the "new" lands under European control and into the Catholic faith. Taken together, these three papal bulls established an explicit theological justification for the legal right to the expropriation of land and the enslavement of non-Christian peoples all over the world. The doctrine of discovery affirmed colonizers and enslavers as agents of God's salvation. It also established legal precedent for centuries to follow.

Beginning with the decision in an 1823 land dispute titled *Johnson v. McIntosh*, the Supreme Court of the United States has repeatedly cited the doctrine of discovery as a legal justification to deny the rights of Native Americans to their land.[9] The unanimous opinion in that case, penned by Chief Justice John Marshall, referred to the established principle that "discovery gave title to the government by whose subjects, or by whose authority, it was made, against all other European governments, which title might be consummated by possession," and argued that the Native Americans' "power to dispose of the soil of their own will, to whomsoever they pleased, was denied by the original fundamental principle, that discovery gave exclusive title to those who made it."[10]

---

8 Charles and Rah, 15.
9 Charles and Rah, 104–28.
10 Charles and Rah, 108.

Johnson v. McIntosh encouraged states to enforce their claims to land by removing Native Americans. In the years following the ruling, Georgia sought to exercise its claim to Cherokee lands. In support of this claim, President Andrew Jackson signed the Indian Removal Act in 1830, which laid the foundation for the forced removal of Cherokees and others that came to be known as the Trail of Tears. *Johnson v. McIntosh* and its appeal to the doctrine of discovery would continue to be cited as legal precedent into the twenty-first century. In cases in 1954, 1985, and 2005, the court referred to the case and to the doctrine of discovery to deny Native American groups' attempts to reclaim lands lost by force or illegal purchase.

The history of the doctrine of discovery is far more complex and contentious than this brief overview suggests. Its earliest origins can be said to go back to early Christian imperialism in the eighth century, to the crusades in the eleventh, and to the medieval Christian construction of Jews as inferior.[11] The bulls were part of the popes' efforts to adjudicate the claims of European nations to the newly "discovered" territories. They were primarily directed toward Portugal and Spain— two Roman Catholic nations that were themselves constructed as nonwhite from an English Protestant perspective.[12] The doctrine of discovery stands as one event in a long process of the ideological construction of whiteness and the systems of colonialism, racism, and slavery. In this sense, it is neither the origin of whiteness nor its culmination. It is, however, an event that epitomizes how those constructions emerge from theological soil. Accordingly, my purpose in considering it here is not primarily historical, either to trace the whole history of the doctrine or to argue for its decisive importance. Rather, my purpose is ideological, to use the doctrine to show how the construction of whiteness is a profound theological distortion. It is a

---

11 M. Lindsay Kaplan, *Figuring Racism in Medieval Christianity* (Oxford: Oxford University Press, 2019).

12 Carla E. Roland Guzmán, "Dismantling the Discourses of the 'Black Legend' as They Still Function in the Episcopal Church: A Case against Latinx Ministries as a Program of the Church," *Anglican Theological Review* 101, no. 4 (October 1, 2019): 603–24.

distortion that continues to shape theology—including environmental theology—from its foundations.

II. WHITENESS AS IDOLATRY

The dominant category in *Romanus Pontifex* and the other papal bulls implicated in the doctrine of discovery is not race but rather religion. The worldview established here is one divided into faithful and infidel. Likewise, while they do refer to racial categories, the bulls are not unique or novel in this regard. What is significant, though, is that by overlaying the religious schema onto the racial schema, the popes take a significant step in the construction of whiteness by establishing black and white as markers of ontology (that is, of being) and soteriology (of salvation). With these documents, the doctrine of discovery reconfigures soteriology along racially constructed lines, with whiteness as the defining category.[13]

According to Willie James Jennings, the encounter with new worlds in the time of the bulls occasioned a crisis for the church. The church's philosophical and theological authority was called into question as established doctrines of creation seemed unable to account for previously unimagined geographies and unknown peoples.[14] In this context, a racialized hierarchy of creation (and salvation) imposed a knowable and controllable order on this newly transformed world. Categories of color provided an interpretive scheme into which new peoples and places could be placed: the darker bodies of new lands, whether in Africa or the Americas, were essentially interchangeable in their inferiority to white bodies.[15] All other realities of their cultures or places were wiped out by this single totalizing category. In this scheme, whiteness emerges as the conceptual center around which all other peoples and places are

---

13 Willie James Jennings, *The Christian Imagination: Theology and the Origins of Race* (New Haven, CT: Yale University Press, 2011), 27–38.

14 Jennings, *The Christian Imagination*, 84–88.

15 Jennings, 30.

organized. The white body is the implicit norm; it represents value, civilization, and refinement. The value of other bodies is determined by their perceived proximity to whiteness. This hierarchy functions conceptually as a way to understand these new realities, and it functions materially by controlling and abusing those bodies that sit lower on the scale of value.

As *Romanus Pontifex* illustrates, it also functions soteriologically: it transposes categories of election and salvation onto the racial hierarchy. Jennings cites Pope Nicholas's account of the exploits of Prince Henry, where he notes the "many Guineamen and other negroes, taken by force," who "have been converted to the Catholic faith," before expressing the hope that "by the help of divine mercy . . . either those peoples will be converted to the faith or at least the souls of many of them will be gained for Christ."[16] In a few lines, Nicholas renders a broad and diverse range of peoples and places as one monolithic group, defined by two characteristics: their skin color and their need for salvation (by white Europeans). This, then, is what is distinctive about the doctrine of discovery and its historical moment: through a process that was simultaneously theological and political, skin color was established as the primary ontological and soteriological organizing principle for understanding humanity. In Jennings's words, "Europeans enacted racial agency as a theologically articulated way of understanding their bodies in relation to new spaces and new peoples and to their new power over those spaces and peoples."[17]

In this respect, the doctrine of discovery is one moment that exemplifies the broader development of whiteness as a theological distortion. It is not the first such moment, nor is it unique. In fact, it is important precisely because it is one among many such claims within a process that spans centuries. What is distinctive about the doctrine, however, is how clearly it demonstrates how whiteness distorts theology.

---

16 Jennings, 27.
17 Jennings, 58.

The theological problems here are many. But the primary distortion that occurs in this process is displacement, the severing of theology from the earth and places. The identities of peoples, previously a function of their places and cultures, are translated into aesthetic categories that transcend all particularities. Lands and peoples become fungible commodities, resources to be exploited, rather than irreducible features of creation. Creation itself ceases to be an act of God, who creates a wealth of diverse places and peoples, and instead becomes the prerogative of European colonizers, who have the power to claim and reconfigure spaces according to their purposes. While the implications of this distortion extend far beyond theologies of creation, their direct significance for creation care and Christian environmentalism are clear.

The problem, however, runs deeper than a flawed theology of creation, with all its disastrous ecological and human consequences. The fundamental theological error, according to Jennings, is supersessionism: this displacement violates the central narrative of salvation in Scripture, which is the story of God's relationship with Israel. For Christians, the salvation that Christ mediates is the continuation of a story that begins with God's election of Israel in a particular place. God chooses Israel and places them in the promised land. Of course, the fact that in doing so God appears to sanction the violent removal of those already inhabiting the land represents another theological problem. There is no simple way of explaining away this violence. What it certainly cannot entail, though, is a transferrable justification for similar violent acts of conquest.[18] Again, God's particular history with Israel remains decisive and unrepeatable. The salvation that Jesus, a Jew, promises does not replace God's election of Israel but extends Israel's election to Gentiles through him.[19] This gives rise, for Jennings, to a theology of communion as joining in place, being grafted onto the people of God, which I will consider further below.

---

18 Jennings, 257–58.
19 Jennings, 262.

The colonialist distortion abstracts election from the people and land of Israel and constructs it as a property of whiteness. Instead of the body of Jesus, this supersessionist theology centers on the white European body.[20] The supposed salvation that is mediated by this white body happens in any place and no place; places lose their significance as a part of God's story of salvation, and they become mere commodities or resources. The possibility of real communion as the joining of diverse peoples—the "nations" of Scripture—is eliminated, since the peoples are robbed of the irreducible particularity that comes from being in and of a particular place.

This theological production of whiteness resembles the historical heresy of Docetism. Docetism was the belief, rejected at the First Council of Nicaea in 325, that denied the reality of Christ's materiality, arguing that Christ only appeared to be human. In one sense, the colonial construction of whiteness resembles Docetism in the way it replaces the role of the body of Christ in salvation with the white European body. Christ's soteriological significance is translated from a particular Jewish human being to the ideal of the white body. As in Docetism, Christ's physical body, with its historical particularity, is denied in favor of an abstraction—in this case, the category of whiteness. This construction of whiteness also resembles Docetism in the way it denies the incarnation of other bodies, as nonwhite and nonhuman bodies are robbed of their individuality and seen only as instances of broader racial categories. Physical bodies are again replaced by ideological categories.

In its Docetic and supersessionist aspects, whiteness distorts theology by denying the incarnation. By replacing Christ's body as the locus of salvation with a white European body, whiteness distorts the reality of God incarnate in a particular, historical (dark-skinned) human body. Yet the more radical theological distortion at work is idolatry.[21] Whiteness, rather than Christ, is established as the center of creation and redemption. Salvation is understood with respect not

---

20 Jennings, 286.
21 I am grateful to an anonymous reviewer for this insight.

to God's saving action in Christ but rather in the actions of white Europeans. Whiteness becomes an idol.

Addressing patriarchy and sexism, Brazilian ecofeminist Ivone Gebara offers a description of the idolatrous character of oppressive systems that also encompasses this idolatrous whiteness. In her astute analysis of evil from the perspective of women's suffering, she names the evils of "asserting the superiority of one sex over the other, superiority that permeates social, political, cultural, and religious structures," and "making people believe that one knows the will of God, that one can teach it or even impose it," as well as "exploiting the earth as an object of profit . . . to the detriment of the life of entire peoples." She identifies these evils with the idolatry of being "white, male, racially pure, of belonging to the chosen people."[22]

As Gebara's contemporary analysis demonstrates, just as the legal ramifications of the doctrine of discovery have persisted into the twenty-first century, so too has its heretical and idolatrous construction of whiteness. Kelly Brown Douglas identifies the theological concept of whiteness at the heart of what she calls "stand-your-ground culture." Douglas locates the historical trajectory of this theological construction in a slightly different process from Jennings: the creation of a myth of Anglo-Saxon exceptionalism, first in England and subsequently in the American colonies. An ethnographic myth of a distinctive European race laid the foundation for the colonizers' sense of divine mission to be God's chosen people in a "new" land.[23] As in Jennings's account, whiteness takes on theological significance in a hierarchy of salvation; whiteness is associated with election, and nonwhiteness with sin.[24]

The nineteenth-century expression of this myth was "manifest destiny," the doctrine (closely related to the doctrine of discovery) that invokes divine providence to justify violence against nonwhite

---

22 Ivone Gebara, *Longing for Running Water: Ecofeminism and Liberation*, trans. David Molineaux (Minneapolis: Fortress Press, 1999), 139.

23 Douglas, *Stand Your Ground*, 16.

24 Douglas, 42–43.

peoples to expand and protect white spaces and privileges.[25] The twentieth- and twenty-first-century expression of Anglo-Saxon exceptionalism, Douglas says, is stand-your-ground culture. Stand-your-ground culture takes its name from the law in many jurisdictions that allows certain individuals to use violence to protect their space, a law that was invoked (though not as a formal defense) to justify the 2012 killing of unarmed Black teenager Trayvon Martin. As opposed to the law itself, Douglas's concept of stand-your-ground culture refers to "the social-cultural climate that makes the destruction and death of black bodies inevitable and even permissible."[26] It is the network of cultural assumptions and explicit policies that allow and even encourage the construction and protection of white spaces and privileges through violence.

Whiteness remains a theological problem as much as a political and social one. Even when they have not been overtly racist, contemporary predominantly white churches have nevertheless been reluctant to address whiteness and white supremacy in the past and in the present. When predominantly white churches are unwilling and unable to identify the suffering of people of color with Jesus's own suffering on the cross, they simply do not see the reality of the cross. Failing to envision Jesus as a person of color in North America means failing to see him at all, says Douglas, "for in a context brimming with Anglo-Saxon white supremacy, the crucified Jesus is simply not white."[27] Whiteness is fundamentally opposed to the freedom that God intends for all of creation. It opposes blackness, and so, according to Douglas, it opposes the reality of the crucified Christ. Whiteness stands with the crucifiers.

For Jennings, too, the modern-day distortion of whiteness opposes Christ and the new life of communion he offers, subsuming him into the "social imaginations of nations." Christ and salvation are reconfigured as possessions of peoples, rather than peoples reconfiguring

---

25 Douglas, 108–9.
26 Douglas, xiii.
27 Douglas, 201.

their lives and imaginations in conformity to him.[28] Beyond this, though, this distortion also separates us and our lives from the land. Where God promises a transformation of peoples in a new communion that includes and embraces their identities and places, whiteness and colonialism abstract peoples from those identities and places and transform them into racial identities. Contemporary theologies perpetuate this idolatrous whiteness when they read creation accounts as if they are addressed directly to (white) Christians, rather than to the Israelites. They perpetuate it when they implicitly privilege white experiences of God or (for environmental theologies especially) of creation, forgetting that God has addressed and continues to address peoples in their particularity, in the depth of their cultural expression, and in and through the concrete reality of specific places. They perpetuate it when they do not clearly and directly examine and excise the assumptions of whiteness embedded in their theological claims, representations of God, and liturgical practices. And they perpetuate heretical whiteness, especially in its associations with Docetism, when they offer lip service to overcoming historical and present-day racism and colonialism but fail to incarnate these words with concrete steps toward racial and environmental justice and reparations.

Again, this has grave consequences for theologies of creation and Christian environmentalism. By establishing whiteness as the dominant interpretive lens through which theology, like society more broadly, views the world, this colonialist logic robs places and peoples of their distinctiveness, their particularity, as creatures of God. This logic makes it impossible for a culture formed by whiteness to approach these peoples and places with anything approaching care or love, as farmer and agrarian author Wendell Berry saw over four decades ago in his seminal book *The Unsettling of America*. "One of the peculiarities of the white race's presence in America," says Berry, "is how little intention has been applied to it. As a people, wherever

---

28 Jennings, *The Christian Imagination*, 292.

we have been, we have never really intended to be."[29] As Jennings demonstrates, this lack of intentionality is not merely a byproduct of a careless culture; rather, it reflects a racist theological distortion at its political and economic foundations.

III. WAYS OF KNOWING IN THE GAPS

So far in this chapter, I have shown how the whiteness of Christian environmentalism represents a profound theological problem—both heretical and idolatrous—as it displaces creation theology by separating people from their places, distorts soteriology by separating people from one another and from God's promise of communion, and misrepresents Christ by failing to see his crucifixion in the suffering of nonwhite peoples. For ecotheology to overcome this distortion, however, it is necessary to see that the problem lies not only in the theological content (what we believe about God) but in our theological method (how we think about God). In other words, it is an epistemological problem. The remainder of this chapter is concerned with how we first understand and, second, begin to solve this epistemological problem.

Epistemology is the study or philosophy of knowledge; it is sustained reflection on how we know anything at all, and what we mean when we claim to know something. Thus, to say that whiteness is an epistemological problem is to say that whiteness shapes how we think, how we claim to know things, and what we consider to be legitimate forms of knowledge. Recall that, in the previous chapter, I suggested that scientific forms of knowledge can be limited and narrow, excluding, for example, Indigenous ways of knowing. This is an epistemological concern. Here, I want to show that ecotheology and Christian environmentalism are subject to similar epistemological limitations—limitations that stem from whiteness.

---

29 Wendell Berry, *The Unsettling of America: Culture & Agriculture*, reprint ed. (Berkeley: Counterpoint, 2015), 5.

Whiteness has always been an epistemological project. Europeans' earliest encounters with the "new" world occasioned what Jennings, borrowing from Andean culture, calls *pachacuti*, the "world turned upside down": a cataclysmic upheaval that challenged the received knowledge of both civilizations.[30] The Europeans undertook the task of constructing new frames of interpretation to accommodate this new reality. In sixteenth-century Peru, this task fell largely to a Jesuit theologian and educator named José de Acosta, and the political-theological scheme that he constructed exemplifies the epistemological project of colonialism.[31] His book *Historia general de las Indias* is a comprehensive description of the new world interpreted through the natural law theology of the old world, which saw God's eternal law reflected in the ordering of creation and in human nature. Acosta attempted to reconcile the realities of the Americas with the doctrines of the church, especially the doctrine of creation, so he was forced to reckon with questions like how such diverse peoples could have descended from one ancestor, or how so many species of animals could have dispersed so widely after leaving Noah's ark. He also addressed the question of how God's providence extended to this new non-Christian world: "Our Eternal Lord has enriched the most remote parts of the world [with mineral wealth] in order to invite men to seek out and possess those lands and coincidentally to communicate their religion and the worship of the one true God."[32] In other words, he believed that God mobilized the colonizers' desire for wealth to enact the goal of the conversion of the Indigenous peoples of the Americas. For Acosta, salvation and economic colonization were linked, not only in the agency of the colonizers but in God's providential plan.

Accordingly, Acosta devised a hierarchy of peoples, sorting the "barbarians" of various continents according to their capability for civilization and salvation. As a Jesuit, a member of a religious order

---

30 Jennings, *The Christian Imagination*, 72.
31 Jennings, 82–116.
32 Jennings, 92.

of educators, Acosta was directly interested in conversion and theological formation. The joining of economic colonization with conversion and salvation meant that "the operation of forming productive workers for the mines, encomiendas, haciendas, the obrajes, and the reducciones merged with the operation of forming theological subjects."[33] So Acosta's hierarchy constructed a racialized scheme whereby peoples were grouped according to their ability to learn to be more economically productive and simultaneously more Christian, all by becoming more like the colonizers—that is, by becoming more white. Here, his encyclopedic production of theological-scientific knowledge about the new world becomes a way of establishing and exercising power over the peoples of that world. Crucially, the idea that the Indigenous peoples had their own forms of knowledge and ways of understanding the world had no place in Acosta's system; it was white knowledge that was definitive. The economic and political operations of whiteness in the new world depended on Acosta's epistemological task of producing and promulgating his "knowledge" of it and its peoples.

Whiteness depended on similar epistemological work to justify slavery and racism in the United States. Again a joint effort of natural law theology and the science of the eighteenth, nineteenth, and early twentieth centuries produced a theological-scientific ideology that claimed to provide evidence of the inferiority of Black people and others constructed as nonwhite. God had created Black people to be slaves, it was argued, and for them to be free would violate God's order and their own nature. Nineteenth-century Swiss biologist Louis Agassiz argued that the diversity of human beings necessarily required multiple, discrete creations, a conclusion that he claimed was both scientifically and theologically sound.[34] In his 1885 book *Our Country: Its Possible Future and Its Present Crisis*, Protestant clergyman Josiah Strong marshaled scientific support for the ideology of manifest destiny, drawing on Charles Darwin's theory of natural

33 Jennings, 107.
34 Douglas, *Stand Your Ground*, 63.

selection to argue for the natural and spiritual superiority of Anglo-Saxons and the inevitable assimilation or extinction of all others.[35]

On one level, these arguments are simply claims about Black, white, and brown bodies. Yet on another level, they are claims about knowledge, and about what kinds of knowledge count as legitimate, and this is what makes them an epistemological project. The theological-scientific systems that Acosta, Agassiz, Strong, and so many others helped create were totalizing: they purported to comprehend every aspect of the peoples and places they catalogued, and they excluded any other ways of knowing them (including those of the peoples themselves). And for them it was precisely this totalizing use of reason that demonstrated their superiority. In their minds, and in the natural law theology they inhabited, reason was the noblest human characteristic, the faculty by which human beings participated in God's eternal law. In ordering society along racial lines, these totalizing systems of knowledge performed the natural law, God's will, and simultaneously performed the supposed superiority of whiteness as an ordering, organizing knowledge. As decolonial philosopher Walter Mignolo argues, "confronted with previously unknown groups of people, the colonizing Christians in the Indias Occidentales . . . began determining individuals on the basis of their relation to theological principles of knowledge, which were taken as superior to any other system around the world."[36] This is whiteness as an epistemological project.

One way to understand this kind of epistemological project is through philosopher Michel Foucault's term "power/knowledge." For Foucault, knowledge is always constrained by the limitations of its social context, so power has a role in producing knowledge. At the same time, knowledge of human beings—specifically of different kinds of human bodies—can be a way of controlling them, so that knowledge is a way of producing and maintaining social power.[37] The

---

35 Douglas, 93–94.
36 Cited in Jennings, *The Christian Imagination*, 87.
37 Gary Gutting, *Foucault: A Very Short Introduction* (Oxford: Oxford University Press, 2005), 50–51.

single term "power/knowledge," then, indicates the way knowledge and power are unified in "the deployment of force and the establishment of truth."[38] In the cases of colonialism and slavery, we can see how the theological and political authority of the colonial enterprise, vested in rulers like Prince Henry and priests like Acosta, and that of slavery, exemplified by Strong, produced supposedly objective knowledge of the superiority of whites over those constructed as nonwhite. That knowledge, in turn, classified and objectified those nonwhite bodies in order to control them through racist policies.

One of Foucault's main objectives in describing the operations of power/knowledge is to demonstrate the contingency of knowledge. What is presented as necessary knowledge, specifically the knowledge used to justify institutions or practices like slavery, is in fact the product of a particular social-historical context and its power structures.[39] With respect to whiteness, Foucault's concept, paired with careful analyses like those of Douglas and Jennings, demonstrates that there is nothing inevitable about the idea of whiteness and the normative categories it establishes in its orbit.

Foucault's analysis is important here, because even if Acosta's or Strong's particular claims and categories now seem obsolete, their way of thinking is still with us, in the forms of whiteness I have been describing: the various ways white experiences and perspectives remain the implicit norm, against which all other perspectives are evaluated. The dominant form of knowledge in contemporary academic discourse, including theology, is broadly the same one in which Acosta, Agassiz, Strong, and others operated, and the same one Foucault described. It is rationalist, governed by narrowly conceived rules of logic, and above all it is analytical, in the sense of separating things into component parts. Like Acosta's hierarchy, it distinguishes between fields; between subjects; between categories of things, places, and people; and—crucially—understands those distinctions to be real, not just conceptual tools; and the categories and beings they

---

38 Gutting, *Foucault*, 86.
39 Gutting, 50.

separate to be discrete entities.[40] Then, of course, it evaluates these entities, either implicitly or explicitly establishing a hierarchy of value among them. This knowledge is totalizing, aiming at universal claims rather than plural and partial truths.[41] And as Foucault reminds us, it is powerful: it exercises power over bodies, human and nonhuman. By establishing its categories as real and seemingly self-evident, it can treat beings as interchangeable resources rather than uniquely valuable parts of a related whole.

Gebara has compellingly described the androcentric (male-centered) and anthropocentric (human-centered) ways of knowing inherent in Christian theology.[42] She takes specific aim at the natural law approach, with its affirmation of universal truths and its resulting dependence on existing patriarchal power structures to protect these eternal doctrines.[43] Moreover, this natural law theology operates out of an essentialist framework that posits an immutable human nature, one that inevitably reflects the cultures out of which it arises.[44] These dynamics can easily be seen in the historical examples I have described, with whiteness serving as the ideal expression of that immutable nature, and the church and colonial powers serving as the guardians of universal law. Gebara's point, of course, is that this dogmatism and essentialism remain central to dominant theology.

Similarly, Vine Deloria Jr. sees a theological doctrine of history at the root of colonialist forms of knowledge. For Western Christianity, particularly in the natural law tradition, history is linear and impersonal, as opposed to the more cyclical and embodied accounts of many Indigenous groups.[45] History in Christian theology is the progressive unfolding of a divine purpose—a purpose that eventually came to be centered on the political and cultural destiny of European countries. This linear conception of history is so deeply embedded

---

40 Mignolo and Walsh, *On Decoloniality*, 148; cf. Jennings, *After Whiteness*.
41 Mignolo and Walsh, *On Decoloniality*, 164.
42 Gebara, *Longing for Running Water*, 19–48.
43 Gebara, 43.
44 Gebara, 32–33.
45 Deloria, *Spirit and Reason*, 295.

in Western ways of thinking, theological and secular, that it seems completely natural, even inevitable.

Yet there is nothing inevitable about this way of knowing: alternative epistemologies are possible. Queer theory and queer theology, for example, have shown how those experiences of gender and sexuality that have been constructed as divergent can challenge dominant forms of knowledge. The notion of queerness extends far beyond questions of gender and sex "to suggest that life is much stranger, much more complex than our concepts and language can imagine."[46] This embrace of strangeness and complexity can reshape the very foundations of, among other things, our environmental goals.

At the same time, though, it is not as simple as somehow opting out of the dominant epistemology. The power/knowledge forms of colonialism are so pervasive in the contemporary world that there is no possibility of somehow escaping them or standing outside them in order to critique them.[47] They are the epistemological waters in which we all swim. The only real possibility, then, is to seek the interstices, the fissures or gaps within the dominant forms. Many authors suggest ways of knowing that have this character, and it is worth exploring this constellation of images and its implications for creating more liberating ways of knowing.

Jennings, for example, describes the fragmentation that is intrinsic to the work of theology in a colonial world. Not all fragmentation is bad; faith itself is made up of fragments—stories, sayings, texts, traditions—that believers weave together.[48] But there are forms of fragmentation that come from colonialism and its division and commodification of peoples and lands. The work of theological formation and knowledge begins with these fragments, and with fragmented people, working with them with the aim of communion. Jennings worries about theology that ignores the fragments and instead promotes self-sufficiency, making that genuine communion impossible.

---

46 Whitney A. Bauman and Kevin J. O'Brien, *Environmental Ethics and Uncertainty: Wrestling with Wicked Problems* (Abingdon, UK: Routledge, 2019), 20.

47 Mignolo and Walsh, *On Decoloniality*, 108.

48 Jennings, *After Whiteness*, 32.

Christian environmental ethicist Willis Jenkins uses a similar image when he argues that ethics should arise "from the scene of a wound": it should begin with concrete social problems and the innovative, emergent strategies communities form to respond to them.[49] This leads to a pragmatic approach to ethics that focuses on practical innovation and problem solving rather than theorizing about worldviews. In addition to emerging from a wound, an urgent social problem, this pragmatic approach to ethics relies on another generative gap: the gap between the limits of our current moral abilities and the demands of immense problems like climate change or species extinction.[50] The work of theological ethics within these gaps begins by reinterpreting them Christologically, insisting on the promise of reconciliation through and behind the brokenness and suffering of the world.[51] By understanding the world's wounds in light of the cross, Christian theological ethics can affirm God's solidarity and transforming presence within them. Like Jennings's fragments, Jenkins uses the image of wounds or gaps to argue for new methods, new forms of ethical and theological thinking that begin from real, complex experiences and accept ambiguity and incompleteness.

Perhaps no writer has better exemplified this decolonial notion of thinking in the gaps or wounds better than Gloria Anzaldúa. Anzaldúa's work famously resists simple classification—indeed, this is part of her decolonial praxis. A queer Chicana (a term of empowerment claimed by persons of Mexican descent born in the United States) feminist writer, she intentionally subverts the narrowness of dominant epistemologies by combining poetry, essays, personal reflection, and even sketches in her work, and by shifting fluidly from English to Spanish, often without translation. Her writing draws heavily on postcolonial and feminist philosophy, queer theory, Indigenous worldviews, spirituality, and even some theology, though she is critical of traditional Christian doctrine. In her seminal book *Borderlands/La Frontera:*

---

49 Jenkins, *The Future of Ethics*, 82, 94.
50 Jenkins, 95.
51 Jenkins, 98.

The New Mestiza, she uses the image of the border to represent a new kind of consciousness, one characterized by ambiguity rather than certainty, inclusive holism rather than divisiveness, and change rather than stability. The US–Mexico border, she says, is "una herida abierta," an open wound, "where the Third World grates against the first and bleeds . . . the lifeblood of the two merging to form a third country—a border culture."[52] Her notion of the consciousness of the borderlands, which she also describes as *mestiza* consciousness, has influenced many decolonial authors' arguments for new forms of knowledge that cross boundaries to embrace pluralism and ambiguity.[53]

It is Anzaldúa's posthumously published final work, though, that most completely describes and even enacts radically new ways of knowing. In *Light in the Dark/Luz en lo Oscuro: Rewriting Identity, Spirituality, Reality,* she relies less on the image of the borderlands and more on Mexican Indigenous images and terms. She uses the Nahuatl word *nepantla* to identify a space of liminal or transitional consciousness—the gaps or wounds I have been describing. "Wounding," she says, citing writer Jean Houston, "is the entrance to the sacred."[54] Yet she also speaks more directly of wounds: her central image for the titular "light in the dark" is the Aztec goddess of the moon, Coyolxauhqui (Ko-yol-sha-UH-kee), who was decapitated by her brother, her body broken into a thousand pieces, traditionally depicted by a round stone covered with dismembered body parts.[55] For Anzaldúa, Coyolxauhqui represents the necessary epistemological journey of fragmentation, wounding, and transformative healing.

What is so powerful about Anzaldúa's description of this journey is the way she inhabits this interstitial space: rather than simply

---

52 Gloria Anzaldúa, *Borderlands/La Frontera: The New Mestiza,* 4th ed. (San Francisco: Aunt Lute Books, 2012), 25.

53 Anzaldúa, *Borderlands,* 99–101; Mignolo and Walsh, *On Decoloniality,* 145–50.

54 Gloria Anzaldúa, *Light in the Dark/Luz en lo Oscuro: Rewriting Identity, Spirituality, Reality,* ed. AnaLouise Keating, illustrated ed. (Durham, NC: Duke University Press, 2015), 153.

55 Anzaldúa, *Light in the Dark,* xxi, 124.

write about alternative, nonrational or nondominating ways of knowing, she writes from within them.[56] Thus, when she speaks of Indigenous ideas—like the *naguala*, the Nahuatl word for a shape-shifter, which represents the creative process; *el cenote*, a sinkhole that was a Mayan sacrificial site and connects us to other realities; or *el árbol de la vida*, the tree of life that similarly bridges different realms—she does not reject the possibility that these are genuine realities.[57] In fact, she explicitly argues that "nonliteral realities, such as chamanas' [shamans'] flights to other worlds," are simply another reality. "Imagination," she insists, is "not . . . a marginal nonreality nor...an altered state but, rather, . . . another type of reality."[58] She experienced the natural world as ensouled, as a source of sacred communication.[59] She describes personal experiences of physical and emotional trauma, out-of-body experience, dreams, and drug use, all to demonstrate the reality of this liminal *nepantla* conscious-ness.[60] Anzaldúa's struggle against dominant ways of knowing and thinking was not an abstraction; it was a life-or-death effort to inhabit different, at times conflicting, realities. We will consider the force of this decolonial, reality-transforming consciousness further in the next chapter.

These images—gaps, fragments, borders, wounds—are not the same, nor are they necessarily describing precisely the same kind of approach. What they share, though, is the claim that in the face of the totalizing knowledge of colonialism, alternative knowledges must be sought in liminal spaces—spaces of transition, movement, or trauma. They must be sought in the dynamic points of contact between worlds, where identities and worldviews encounter each other and sometimes conflict. And as a result, they must be ways of knowing that are comfortable with ambiguity, paradox, and tension.

---

56 Anzaldúa, xxix.
57 Anzaldúa, 25.
58 Anzaldúa, 37.
59 Anzaldúa, 117.
60 Anzaldúa, 134–35.

IV. BORDERLANDS: TOWARD AN ANTI-OPPRESSIVE METHOD FOR ECOTHEOLOGY

In the town of Nogales, which straddles the US–Mexico border in Arizona and Sonora, La Casa de la Misericordia y de Todas las Naciones offers food, shelter, and services to migrants trying to enter the United States. It attracts volunteers and pilgrims, including artists, craftspeople, clergy, social workers, medical and legal professionals, and scholars. When musician Joe Troop spent a month at the shelter, offering migrants music lessons and friendship, he was moved by both the struggle and the compassion he witnessed.[61] Troop wrote the song "Mercy for Migrants," which he subsequently recorded with banjo players Abigail Washburn and Bela Fleck, and which was featured in an article in *Rolling Stone* magazine.[62] The chorus of the song asks,

Who's gonna send for your mother
Longing for her son?
Why aren't we there for each other?
Mercy is for everyone.[63]

From Troop's music to murals to legal expertise and trauma psychology, La Casa de la Misericordia y de Todas las Naciones gathers together a stunning array of different ways of knowing: embodied as well as theoretical, emotional as well as intellectual, placed-based as well as abstract. For many migrants, caring for the shelter's *huertos*

---

61 Egan Millard, "Musician Joe Troop Releases Song, Video Inspired by Episcopal-Supported Migrant Shelter," *Episcopal News Service* (blog), September 20, 2021, https://www.episcopalnewsservice.org/2021/09/20/musician-joe-troop-releases-song-video-inspired-by-episcopal-supported-migrant-shelter/.
62 Jon Freeman, "Che Apalache's Leader Joe Troop Pleads for Empathy in New Song 'Mercy for Migrants,'" *Rolling Stone,* August 11, 2021, accessed October 28, 2021, https://www.rollingstone.com/music/music-country/joe-troop-che-apalache-mercy-for-migrants-1210570/.
63 Joe Troop, "Mercy for Migrants," performed by Joe Troop, Bela Fleck, and Abigail Washburn, from *Borrowed Time* (Free Dirt Records, 2021).

(gardens) brings calm and a sense of connection to the land, and to home. A labyrinth was recently constructed and dedicated on the grounds, and residents and volunteers have walked the *viacrucis,* or Stations of the Cross, along the border. In addition, this eclectic epistemological atmosphere reflects the influence of the Xi-iui and Tohono O'odham Indigenous communities, who, like Anzaldúa, see a relational and personal cosmos, with earth and stars and human and nonhuman species as one connected whole. This embodied and emplaced ecological holism is a source of resistance to the divisiveness of the border itself: migrants there affirm that "la frontera nos divide, pero la tierra nos une [the border divides us, but the land unites us]."[64]

The diverse epistemologies of La Casa de la Misericordia y de Todas las Naciones exemplify, I believe, the kind of decolonial knowing, knowing in the gaps, that I have been describing. At the border, the open wound where worlds grate against one another, a variety of ways of knowing emerge in community. Emotional and artistic forms of knowledge stand alongside scholarly and intellectual knowledge and embodied ecological knowledge, all occasioned by and yet simultaneously resisting the colonial power/knowledge production of the border.

In the next chapter, I will suggest some new theological directions for an anti-oppressive Christian environmentalism. Here, with the powerful image of La Casa de la Misericordia y de Todas las Naciones in mind, I want to establish a foundation for that new ecotheology by identifying some methodological priorities. That is, I want to describe how we might begin to do ecotheology in a way that challenges the dominant epistemology.

The notion of ways of thinking that emerge from gaps, or wounds, or interstitial spaces and embrace ambiguity and paradox will be essential for this task. As the authors I have described demonstrate well, new ways of thinking will not be simply one thing or another; they will not stay in their lane or observe traditional disciplinary

---

64 David Chavez, "Lessons from the Border" (The School of Theology, The University of the South, Sewanee, TN, October 26, 2021).

boundaries. In this section, I will present three characteristics that I think are necessary for decolonial, antiracist theological thinking, and in each of these, there are competing or conflicting impulses. A theological method that challenges colonial thinking will need to hold these competing impulses in tension, standing in the gap or borderland between them, rather than collapsing into one pole or the other.

First, the theological method should be pragmatic, in Jenkins's sense of beginning from lived experience and concrete problems, rather than from theories or worldviews. This meaning of pragmatism is an extension of the approaches of philosophical and moral pragmatism, which began in the United States in the late nineteenth century, and twentieth-century environmental pragmatism. The guiding impulse of moral pragmatism is to eschew the search for absolute truths or foundational commitments, focusing instead on lived experience and moral practices, and attempting to draw conclusions from those sources. Put differently, pragmatism is inductive rather than deductive, bottom-up rather than top-down: it begins from examples of moral claims and seeks generalizable conclusions, rather than identifying fundamental moral principles and then applying those to particular situations.

An illustration may help clarify. When environmental philosopher Bryan Norton served as an advisor to the Environmental Protection Agency (EPA), he quickly observed that the EPA headquarters in Washington, DC was hopelessly convoluted, with various disconnected towers and elevators.[65] This was a result of the rapid but disorganized growth of the agency itself, which, as a matter of political expediency, was born from the consolidation of offices and programs from various other agencies with vastly different philosophies and missions. For Norton, the architectural idiosyncrasies were indicative of the ad hoc organizational structure, which, in turn, pointed to an underlying problem in environmental policy in the

---

65 Bryan G. Norton, *Sustainability: A Philosophy of Adaptive Ecosystem Management*, new ed. (Chicago: University of Chicago Press, 2005), 3.

United States: lack of a shared vocabulary. In public discourse around environmental problems, participants affirm different values and seek different goals, and there is no shared framework or language with which to assess and compare those goals. "What worried me most," he reflects, "was that people from different backgrounds and disciplines continued to interact, carry on conversations, and do their jobs, hardly noticing that they spoke languages without available translations. They, like unattended visitors at the EPA building, wandered into blind corridors and, when they asked how one might get to a more rational environmental policy, they were often told, 'You can't get there from here.'"[66]

As a pragmatist, Norton's proposal is to construct a shared vocabulary centered around the concept of sustainability, not by defining the term in advance but rather by examining how it is used by the different participants in environmental discourse.[67] Sustainability, he argues, is specific enough to have real empirical content—it can be indexed to concrete scientific data—while being broad enough to admit of a variety of evaluative interpretations about which data matter most. What is distinctively pragmatic about this proposal is Norton's refusal to define sustainability in advance, or indeed ever to define it completely, insisting instead on allowing communities to define it in their environmental practices and goals.

The strengths of this pragmatic approach for theological thinking in the gaps are clear. It arises from the site of a wound: from urgent social problems and different communities' conceptualizations of and responses to those problems. It accepts the complexity and ambiguity that goes with that origin in lived experience. Terms and values (like Norton's sustainability) can be negotiated and renegotiated through practices and habits; there are no fixed absolutes. A pragmatic approach can resist the totalizing impulse of colonial ways of knowing by attending carefully to diverse lived experiences. Such an approach for environmental theology and Christian

---

66 Norton, *Sustainability*, 6.
67 Norton, 39–40.

environmentalism might begin not by articulating an overarching theology of creation but rather by joining with communities engaged in environmental struggles and—crucially—by discerning and supporting the moral, spiritual, and practical resources and values present in those communities.

Yet by beginning from lived social realities, pragmatism runs the risk of reinforcing the status quo. By deriving its values from the existing moral commitments and practices of communities, pragmatism seems unable to challenge pervasive and insidious social pathologies like the white racial frame described in Chapter 2—moral ideologies so ingrained in society that they shape the very ways we define and understand problems themselves. If colonialism and race shape the foundations of our public discourses, then pragmatism, despite its faith in communities' abilities to forge new responses to social and environmental problems, is seemingly incapable of addressing these colonialist foundations. This, then, is where our approach must turn its attention to that other sort of gap—Anzaldúa's *nepantla* consciousness and images like it—for imaginative force.

Pragmatism can overcome its myopia, Jenkins suggests, by attending more to the images, metaphors, and cosmologies that communities—including religious communities—draw on to drive their participation and engagement with the earth. He points to philosopher Cornel West's notion of prophetic pragmatism, a pragmatic approach that engages with marginal perspectives, including religious solidarity with "the wretched of the earth."[68] Pragmatism needs religious and imaginative worldviews because these are precisely the kinds of worldviews from which creative moral thinking emerges. In particular, it needs to focus its attention on the wounds, on the places of suffering and struggle, where the moral values of society are questioned and redefined. Thinkers like Anzaldúa, and

---

68 Jenkins, *The Future of Ethics*, 87; cf. Cornel West, *The American Evasion of Philosophy: A Genealogy of Pragmatism* (Basingstoke: Macmillan, 1989), 233–34.

creative engagements like those at La Casa de la Misericordia, provide enormous resources for pragmatist approaches to reflect on and theorize from.

I am suggesting, then, that our theological method must stand at the border between a pragmatist attention to concrete, lived moral experience and the imaginative and prophetic worldviews that can help interpret and, where necessary, critique that experience. It remains pragmatic in its inductive approach, learning from existing moral praxis and enacted values. Yet it is imaginative and prophetic, because part of what it learns is how different forms of knowing can foster deeper and more creative moral solutions.

The second borderland that characterizes this approach relates to its pluralism. Pragmatism and decolonial thought share the affirmation, against the universalizing and totalizing claims of dominant forms of knowledge, that truth can be plural, arising from a variety of different communities and worldviews. If colonial thought accomplishes its purposes by organizing peoples and places hierarchically according to a single value-scale, with whiteness as the monolithic ideal, then resistance to that form of thought involves affirming a variety of different worldviews and ways of valuing. Building on the pragmatist approach just discussed, a pluralist method for environmental theology would look to different environmental worldviews embodied in concrete communities, affirming the helpful moral practices or ideas that emerge from those contexts. It need not be dogmatic; it can be theologically broad, and even embrace more emotional, embodied, and aesthetic ways of knowing and communicating about God. And like Norton's notion of sustainability, it would seek those points of convergence where different worldviews can communicate about specific commitments or values, while allowing communities to fill in the precise content of those terms in different ways.

Yet there is also an aspect of decolonial thinking that drives toward union, or communion. Anzaldúa's Coyolxauhqui represents wounding and dismemberment, but it also moves toward healing and wholeness. Jennings recognizes that faith exists in the fragments, and that theology works with those fragments, yet its ultimate goal is belonging or communion. How can our theological method be accommodatingly pluralist yet reach toward communion?

Jennings responds to this challenge by pointing to the radical communion made possible in Christ, a communion that does not supersede Israel but stands in continuity with it. Belonging in the body of Christ means a new identity that destabilizes cultural and social identities and draws persons, in their concrete particularity and grounded in their places, into a new "cultural intimacy."[69] Joining in this way means "submersion and submission" in the cultural and geographic world of those who came before, of those who have encountered God in this place before us. Such is the position of "second readers" discussed in the previous chapter.

Land can be an essential component of this reading-after. As Jennings demonstrates thoroughly, land and culture are deeply inter-twined, and colonialism's objectification of and alienation from the land reinforces its objectification and alienation of peoples. The communion of a decolonial approach can be grounded in the land, joining with the land and its more-than-human inhabitants, as well as joining, in deference and humility, with those who have previously known the land and known God in the land. This can remain pluralist, admitting a wide variety of experiences and knowledges, while remaining grounded and joined to one another and to a place. Such belonging is possible—indeed, is only possible—by refusing colonialism's attempts at totalizing universal claims.

Again La Casa de la Misericordia is illustrative: as the saying attests, the border divides, but the land unites. In this place of struggle and imperialist alienation, a tremendous wealth of diverse knowledges and experiences join one another, not with any intention of subjugation or exploitation but to belong to one another. And frequently it is with respect to the land itself where this belonging is expressed, in caring for the grounds and *huertos* of the shelter, constructing the labyrinth, and walking the *viacrucis*—physically

---

69 Jennings, *The Christian Imagination*, 265–75.

and symbolically blending different practices of knowing and caring for the land. This community in a literal borderland expresses well a theology that stands at the border between a broad, inclusive pluralism and a radically grounded intimacy of communion in place.

Finally, this theological method occupies a third borderland. It should be public, oriented toward shared concerns and the common good, yet heterogeneous. Pragmatist approaches to theology like the one outlined so far have given considerable attention to the public character of theology, and this has meant several different things. For some, theology is public if it is focused on issues and values of common concern, the questions of a shared life, and if its ideas and discourse are generally accessible to all, beyond confessional boundaries. In other words, public theology is public in its content (that is, its focus on shared concerns) and in its method (its publicly accessible discourse). In these two traits, then, we can see two different meanings of the word "public": public as opposed to private with respect to content, and public as opposed to parochial with respect to method.[70]

According to this understanding of "public", the early and mid-twentieth century was an era of robust public theology. Figures like Reinhold Niebuhr and his brother H. Richard, Paul Tillich, T. S. Eliot, and C. S. Lewis spoke about issues like war, race, and economics, in public forums and in language that was understood to be generally accessible across society. Journalist Alan Jacobs characterized this sort of public theologian:

> They should be intellectuals who speak the language of other intellectuals, including the most purely secular, but they should also be fluent in the concepts and practices of faith. Their task would be that of the interpreter, the bridger of cultural gaps; of the mediator, maybe even the reconciler. Half a century ago, such figures existed in America:

---

70 Linell E. Cady, *Religion, Theology, and American Public Life* (Albany: SUNY Press, 1993), 65.

serious Christian intellectuals who occupied a prominent place on the national stage.[71]

Yet contemporary proponents of public theology would point out that this prominent, more-or-less unified public theology was possible only because its dominant voices and audiences were so homogeneous: predominantly white, male, and Protestant. Such a public theology is neither likely nor desirable today.

Nearly a century ago, pragmatist philosopher John Dewey articulated a different understanding of the work of public intellectuals. For Dewey, the public—or rather, publics—takes shape as actual communities responding to concrete problems.[72] These publics are emergent, dynamic, and experimental; various forms are possible, and "their value is . . . to be measured by their consequences."[73] The challenge for public intellectuals becomes how, in a divided, scattered society, a "manifold public" can come to define itself and its interests. In other words, "the outstanding problem of the public is discovery and identification of itself."[74] On this view, a theology is public theology if it can create publics: communities able to respond to problems.

Thus a decolonial theological method should be public, but in this dynamic and pluralist sense of diverse and emergent publics, rather than one monolithic public. Some postcolonial thinkers have described this as a vision of "subaltern counterpublics": subordinated groups that emerge as publics, contesting the dominant narratives and renarrating their own identities, interests, and needs.[75] Subaltern counterpublics would not necessarily fit traditional ideas of the

---

71 Alan Jacobs, "The Watchmen," *Harper's Magazine*, September 2016, https://harpers.org/archive/2016/09/the-watchmen/.

72 John Dewey, *The Public and Its Problems* (New York: Henry Holt & Company, 1927), 64.

73 Dewey, *The Public and Its Problems*, 74.

74 Dewey, 185.

75 Nancy Fraser, "Rethinking the Public Sphere: A Contribution to the Critique of Actually Existing Democracy," in *Habermas and the Public Sphere*, ed. Craig Calhoun (Cambridge, MA: The MIT Press, 1992), 123; Benjamin

public, since by definition they redefine what counts as public. They create the public sphere as they enter it, by contesting and negotiating what counts as public concern or publicly accessible discourse. They necessarily expand the public sphere, raising issues and perspectives that were previously excluded.

This, then, is the third borderland of the anti-oppressive theological method I am proposing: the space between a public orientation toward shared concerns and a counterpublic orientation of contestation and struggle against dominant discourses. Environmental justice movements can be seen as counterpublic theology of this sort.[76] They address themselves to matters of urgent concern for our common life, such as pollution, land use, and climate change, yet they are simultaneously emergent, subaltern counterpublics. By "refram[ing] environmental problems as political problems," they renegotiate what counts as environmental goods and harms, and the systems by which those values are distributed.[77] And by mobilizing communities to organize in response to environmental harms, particularly from communities of color and often with women as leaders, they have been instrumental in the formation of new counterpublics.

V. CONCLUSION

The doctrine of discovery and the colonial ideology it represents are not only unjust legal manipulations; they are also an idolatrous theological distortion. They distort doctrines of creation and salvation by organizing persons and places according to a logic of whiteness. They remove salvation history from the narrative of Israel and instead

---

Valentin, *Mapping Public Theology: Beyond Culture, Identity, and Difference* (Harrisburg, PA: Bloomsbury T&T Clark, 2002), 124.

76 Andrew R. H. Thompson, "Environmental Justice as Counterpublic Theology: Reflections for a Postpandemic Public," *American Journal of Theology & Philosophy* 41, no. 2–3 (May 1, 2020): 114–32, https://doi.org/10.5406/amerjtheophil.41.2-3.0114.

77 Jenkins, *The Future of Ethics*, 205.

locate it in the narrative of the white European conquest and genocide of other continents. Nor are these doctrines relics of an earlier
era. The doctrine of discovery still serves as legal precedent for the
continued denial of Native American land claims. More troublingly,
the whiteness at its heart still characterizes the dominant worldviews
of the United States, reflected, for example, in Douglas's "stand-
your-ground culture." And the distortions of whiteness continue to
pervade the theological mainstream.

What makes whiteness so insidious in these discourses is that it
is an epistemological project: it constructs ways of knowing inside of
which whiteness and its basic premises make sense. Theologically, this
has often taken the shape of a type of natural law theology that asserts
an immutable order wherein whiteness, maleness, and rationality are
associated with a superior human nature, and ultimately with God.
The pervasiveness of this epistemological project is precisely what
makes alternative ways of knowing so difficult—and so necessary.

For environmental theology to overcome the whiteness it has
inherited, it must seek not only new ecological and theological
thoughts but radically new ways of thinking ecology and theology.
Queer, feminist, and decolonial theologians, among many others, have
proposed such alternatives: ways of knowing that embrace strangeness and complexity in our thought. In this chapter, I have suggested
three characteristics of a decolonial approach for decolonial environmental theology—characteristics that position this approach in three
different border spaces. The approach should be pragmatic, but with
a prophetic imagination; pluralist, but with an orientation toward
communion; and public, but as multiple emergent counterpublics.

What I have proposed is only a beginning, however. These are
the methodological steps that must be taken if ecotheology is to
attempt to rid itself of the whiteness at its roots. In the next chapter,
I will begin to articulate some of the theological seedlings that might
emerge from a decolonial soil. In particular, I will try to envision
an ecotheology that grows organically from the seeds of Anzaldúa's
radically imaginative *nepantla* consciousness.

CHAPTER 4

Apocalypse, Desire, and Incarnation

A dancer wrapped in billowy red clothes dances passionately, even aggressively, through abandoned airport concourses and empty runways; at one point she seems to be climbing vertically up the tarmac. Jagged rock faces towering over a turbulent sea emerge from a dense white fog, gulls circling on air currents. A child pounds out an angry tune on the low end of a piano while singing an expletive-laden ode to the pandemic (in English). A woman speaks by telephone from behind the picture window of her living room about the time she asked the elf-maiden for permission to move a large boulder and convert it into an art-piece called "This Will Pass," a great carved stone chair next to the river Varmá. Aerial shots show empty highways, soccer fields, and parking lots; and motionless cranes, airplanes, and forklifts; while mournful, eerie vocals sing in Icelandic. One stunning and disorienting image, apparently shot vertically looking down a cliff face toward the ocean, seems to show foamy waves crashing upward against a rock ceiling while a gull glides across the scene.

These are some of the memorable images from the film *Apausalypse*, shot in Iceland during the first peak of COVID-19 in spring of 2020 by filmmakers Anni Ólafsdóttir and Andri Snær Magnason.[1]

---

1 Andri Snær Magnason and Anni Ólafsdóttir, *Apausalypse* (Elsku Run Productions, 2020), https://emergencemagazine.org/film/apausalypse/.

Ólafsdóttir and Magnason wanted to capture the unique moment of "this great pause," when society as a whole simply stopped for weeks, to ask, "What is it showing us?"[2] They interviewed artists, musicians, and philosophers. These interviews are interspersed with images of emptied spaces, human and wild, and performances by the interviewees. By far the most striking of these performances is that of Unnur Elísabet, the dancer in red, shown repeatedly throughout the film as she dances her way through customs, security, shops, kitchens, and empty runways.

The recurring theme that runs through the film is, naturally, that of apocalypse in its different meanings. The abandoned streets and buildings suggest a landscape that is apocalyptic in the familiar sense of the end of human society as we know it. During the pandemic, thoughts of this sense of apocalypse have been hard to avoid; as I write, eighteen months after Ólafsdóttir and Magnason made *Apausalypse* and still quite immersed in the pandemic, those thoughts persist. Meanwhile, the images of stark cliffs and turbulent seas, of wild horses and soaring birds, overlaid with interviewees' meditations on global climate change and the excesses of capitalist society, call to mind the slower, more insistent apocalypse that threatens both human and more-than-human worlds. For the film's subjects, two apocalypses are connected, with COVID-19 serving as a call to consider, once again, the disastrous effects of our way of life. Cellist Gunnar Kvaran reflects, "In my long life, I have learned that when I do not listen to life's warnings, which I always receive when I lose my way; when I do not listen to those warnings, and consider them, things turn out badly." He later adds, "If none of these warnings that life gives to humans are enough, then I feel there is only one thing left in the situation: suffering."[3]

This reflection suggests the other, more precise meaning of apocalypse. Visual artist Haraldur Jónsson points out that the original

---

2 Andri Snær Magnason and Anni Ólafsdóttir, "Apausalypse: Dispatch from Iceland," *Emergence* magazine, May 21, 2020, accessed November 10, 2021, https://emergencemagazine.org/essay/apausalypse-dispatch-from-iceland/.

3 Snær Magnason and Ólafsdóttir, *Apausalypse*, 25:17, 42:10.

Greek meaning of apocalypse is "uncovering."[4] Images throughout the film suggest this other sense of apocalypse as well, such as cliffs emerging from the fog, or two dancers alternatively covered and uncovered by a flowing plastic sheet in the middle of a street. When Gunnar Kvaran reflects on life's warnings, this sense of unveiling is reinforced by footage of a dazzling beam of light shining through gray clouds onto the bank of a river. The premise of the film relies on this bivalence of apocalypse: it asks, in this unprecedented moment, where ideas and images of end times are unavoidable, What truth is being revealed to us?

In this chapter, I want to draw on these images of apocalypse to develop further Gloria Anzaldúa's suggestions of *nepantla* consciousness, exemplified in the dismembered-and-remembered icon of Coyolxauhqui. I will consider similarly liminal, subversive ways of knowing in Scripture: the rich imaginary landscape of biblical apocalyptic, the boundary-crossing portrayals of nature in the Song of Songs, and the paradigmatic instance of transgression in Christian theology, the incarnation.

The apocalypticism of the current ecological moment is, in a sense, what gives shape to these considerations. This is not merely because of the cataclysmic urgency of seemingly world-ending crises but even more because of the sense, again, of unveiling inherent in apocalypse. In biblical apocalypse, of course, these two senses are linked. In apocalypse—and similarly in the urgency of desire in the Song of Songs, and the concrete immediacy of the incarnation—the threat or tension of the moment exceeds the bounds of everyday discourse, revealing new possibilities.[5] The moments that give rise to these three themes push against the limits of normal ways of knowing in two seemingly contrary directions: toward a transcendent reality on an epic scale and toward the immanent reality of bodies. This apparent tension is the ambiguity of *nepantla* at work, destabilizing the boundaries between human and more-than-human, between spirit and

---

4 Snær Magnason and Ólafsdóttir, 9:13.
5 I'm grateful to Collin Cornell for this way of putting it.

matter, and between transcendence and immanence—ultimately showing those boundaries to be illusory.

The goal here is not simply to describe an anti-oppressive ecotheology that is more attentive to these themes of apocalyptic literature, the Song of Songs, or deep incarnation. Rather, it is to suggest that our own apocalyptic moment calls for equally transgressive theological imaginations. The urgency of our time invites a corresponding unveiling. These three themes give an indication of what such transgressive theological imagination might look like, and how it might fulfill the expectations laid out in the previous chapter. They call for new ways of relating to one another across and in defiance of the boundaries produced by whiteness. Above all, what they point to is a new way of embodying theology, as the incarnate eco-political body of Christ. This chapter will conclude by describing the need for such a body, and the next chapter will suggest how it might be gathered.

I. IMAGES OF APOCALYPSE

Even before COVID-19, images and narratives of apocalypse abounded in environmental discourse. Climate change is visualized as melting permafrost, collapsing icebergs, and rising seas, all of which seem to portend nothing less than end times. Writing from the Chukchi Peninsula, on the easternmost edge of Asia and twenty miles north of the Arctic Circle, environmental historian and writer Bathsheba Demuth confronts these apocalyptic narratives:

> The future of this place—and all the loved, life-filled places—are given so often now as prophecies of rupture. Years of historical training mean I cannot see the arc of such stories as neutral. They shape the borders of our minds, and our politics. I want to know: Where does it come from, this narrative of absolute end? And what meaning slinks in with a proclamation of apocalypse?[6]

---

6 Bathsheba Demuth, "Reindeer at the End of the World," *Emergence* magazine, July 5, 2020, accessed November 15, 2021, https://emergencemagazine.org/essay/reindeer-at-the-end-of-the-world/.

Looking to the past as a guide, Demuth considers how Soviet interventions in the Chukchi Peninsula, driven by the Soviet apocalyptic narrative of the death of an old world and the inauguration of a glorious new one, brought a sense of absolutism and confidence in humans' ability to control a wild land. Yet that civilization itself failed—that world ended—and what survived was a combination of Indigenous knowledge and pragmatic improvisation: "At the end of a world, there are no damned or saved souls, only people and other kin to share in the work of making life possible. . . . The trick to surviving was in knowing something about the land and the animals, and in keeping on without certainty."[7] Demuth concludes that apocalyptic narratives lead to certainty, self-importance, and nihilism that disregards the present reality, when what is needed is humility, perseverance, and care.

In contrast, Willis Jenkins ascribes a more constructive role to what he calls "apocalyptic strategies," which mobilize both "the imminent catastrophism in urgent warnings about the worst consequences of climate change, and the symbolic interpretation of the present in light of a revealed future."[8] What such strategies do, he suggests, is "open space for cultural transformation by interpreting the world in terms of its future in God." Like Demuth, he worries that these strategies might simply be too much, adding the "symbolic saturation" of apocalypse to an already overwhelming crisis. This could potentially reinforce a nihilistic sense of helplessness or lead to emergency-type measures that reinforce existing power structures. On the other hand, when deployed by the powerless, apocalypse "fires the imagination to look beyond our inheritances."[9] He looks to the example of how the Crow (or Apsáalooke) people preserved their culture in the face of genocide to ask how hope and meaning are sustained beyond cataclysmic events. In such moments, he suggests, belief in a transcendent good beyond all particular, conditional goods

---

7 Demuth, "Reindeer at the End of the World."
8 Jenkins, *The Future of Ethics*, 48.
9 Jenkins, 49.

allows a community to maintain hope for some unforeseeable, and indeed unimaginable, future possibility. "In catastrophe," he says, "responsibility to the future means sustaining a faith that life can be given back to us, even if we lack the concepts for imagining what that could mean."[10]

In the light of historical accounts like Demuth's, these worries about the symbolic power of apocalypse are warranted. Yet they risk missing the rich complexity of biblical apocalyptic literature. Even Jenkins's constructive assessment of apocalyptic strategies is too narrow: apocalyptic imagery offers more than a vague sense of hope in the unimaginable. In its scope and richness, it can offer some of the imaginative resources we need to conceive a world beyond both environmental crisis and colonial thought. It is in this sense that apocalypse resembles Anzaldúa's *nepantla* consciousness. Recall that for Anzaldúa, this Nahuatl word describes a liminal form of knowing that bridges multiple realities; recall, as well, that Anzaldúa manifested this idea in her own experiences of trauma and altered consciousness, and in her writing, which moves fluidly between languages and genres. In its dynamism and ambiguity, *nepantla* resists the hegemony of colonialist thought—that is, it resists the ways colonialism maintains its dominance by enforcing conformity to narrow ways of thinking and speaking.

Apocalyptic literature performs a similar function to *nepantla*. Far from simply dealing with predictions of the end times (or escha-tology), apocalyptic literature is a broad category that spans worlds, epochs, and genres, often for the purpose of subverting the dominant global (and even specifically imperial) order.[11] What characterizes apocalyptic literature as such is a revelation of a transcendent reality that is "both temporal, as it envisages eschatological salvation, and spatial insofar as it involves another, supernatural world."[12] Human reality is bounded by this transcendent reality and reflects its forces

---

10 Jenkins, 305.
11 John J. Collins, *The Apocalyptic Imagination: An Introduction to Jewish Apocalyptic Literature*, 3rd ed. (Grand Rapids, MI: Eerdmans, 2016), epilogue.
12 Collins, *The Apocalyptic Imagination*, chapter 1.

and influences, culminating in a final definitive judgment upon the world. As John Collins points out, this literature provides guidance and reassurance in the face of crises, and offers a broader context in which to clarify fundamental values.[13] He points to Gerhard von Rad's insistence that apocalyptic literature's understanding of revelation resembles the wisdom tradition more than it does prophecy: it is intended to provide a deeper understanding of contemporary events, rather than a prediction of the future.[14] Collins concludes, "it is a resilient tradition that continues to haunt our imaginations and remains an indispensable resource for making sense of human experience."[15]

If, as I have argued, decolonizing environmental theology requires adopting something like Anzaldúa's liminal *nepantla* consciousness, apocalyptic literature may provide useful imaginative resources. A consideration of the two most prominent apocalypses in the Bible, the books of Daniel and Revelation, reveals texts that are truly transgressive, in the sense of boundary crossing: traversing the borders between heaven and earth, present and future (and past), human and more-than-human, and challenging narrow conceptions of what is real and what is mythical.

The book of Daniel is eclectic. It comprises two distinct sections: chapters 1–6, which contain stories, mostly about Daniel, from the Babylonian and Median empires; and chapters 7–12, which relate Daniel's prophetic visions.[16] The book's internal complexity goes further, however. It is written in both Aramaic and Hebrew. The Greek deuterocanonical text, which is treated as canonical in some Christian traditions, includes additional material: the Prayer of Azariah and the Song of the Three Young Men in chapter 3, and the stories of Susanna and of Bel and the Dragon. The book clearly incorporates themes and material from a wide range of sources and periods, including traditional folktales and ancient Near Eastern

---

13 Collins, chapter 1.
14 Collins, chapter 3.
15 Collins, epilogue.
16 Collins, chapter 3.

myth. Yet the compilation of diverse sources gives them a thematic coherence centered on the relation of the people of Israel to Gentile kings as it is played out on a supernatural stage.

The vision of Daniel 7 is particularly evocative, especially when read with environmental turmoil and climate change in mind. Daniel describes a vision of four beasts rising up from a chaotic sea. The beasts are monstrous: a lion with the wings of an eagle that takes on a human-like shape; a great bear with three tusks; a leopard with four wings and four heads; and the fourth, a beast "different from all the other beasts," with ten horns and iron teeth that devours and tramples everything in its path. These dramatic images draw on traditional motifs and recall creation stories. Here, the winds of heaven stir up the great sea, whereas in Genesis 1:2 the divine wind subdued the sea.[17] Elsewhere, such as in Job 26, the defeat of sea monsters is part of God's act of creation.

In the present context, the four monsters represent four Gentile kingdoms: Babylon, Media, Persia, and Greece, with the horns of the final monster representing the kings of Greece, culminating in the persecution of the Jews by Antiochus Epiphanes.[18] Yet, as Collins argues, to identify the referents of these symbols does not exhaust their meaning. The purpose is not simply to relate that one kingdom will succeed another but rather to convey a sense of the terror of their successive reigns. By drawing on established mythical motifs, Daniel reveals that these monstrous kingdoms are "manifestations of the primordial force of chaos."[19] This portrayal is similar to the New Testament language of "powers and principalities" (for example, Ephesians 6:12), interpreted as the spiritual forces behind earthly authorities.[20] In the vision, the "holy ones of the Most High" are ultimately victorious over the monstrous kingdoms.

Thus, there are various layers of meaning at work in this haunting vision of monsters rising from turbulent seas. This multivocality is

---

17 Collins, chapter 3.
18 Collins, chapter 3.
19 Collins, chapter 3.
20 Collins, chapter 3.

reinforced by the fact that the vision of Daniel 7 is complemented by parallel visions in chapters 8–12 that portray the same events in different ways. Collins suggests that "this use of redundance is crucially important for our understanding of apocalyptic language. It implies that the apocalypses are not conveying a 'literal' or univocal truth that can be expressed precisely in one exclusive way. Rather, they share the poetic nature of myth and allude symbolically to a fullness of meaning that can never be reduced to literalness."[21]

In our contemporary context of environmental turmoil, Daniel's representation of earthly kingdoms as monstrous beasts, of destruction emerging from turbulent seas, and of these forces' ultimate defeat, holds considerable imaginative power. Its relevance for this context goes further, however. The author or authors of Daniel were facing a crisis that challenged the prevailing view of worldly power. Under the persecution of Antiochus Epiphanes, the relationship of Jews to Gentile rulers was destabilized.[22] In order to understand this new reality, the authors incorporated ancient mythical themes into a multilayered, highly imaginative text that served two purposes: (1) to interpret situations beyond their control as manifestations of a supernatural conflict, and (2) to articulate a sense of hope that transcended that earthly reality. The hopes that emerge from apocalyptic literature, like the threats that give rise to them, resist being comprehended by any conventional, this-worldly perspective.

The New Testament book of Revelation (from whose Greek title the term "apocalyptic" is derived) is similarly replete with natural and supernatural images juxtaposed in a mythical collage that is saturated with multiple meanings and rich with imperial critique. Considered the most anti-imperial text in the Bible, Revelation takes the form of a letter to Christians in the colonized province of Asia Minor in the Roman Empire from an author who identifies himself as John. John recounts a vision that came to him while he was on the island of Patmos (exiled as a result of his proclamation of the Gospel, according to

---

21 Collins, chapter 3.
22 Collins, chapter 3.

tradition, which scholars find credible).[23] The book draws on Old Testament texts like Daniel and Ezekiel, as well as other mythical sources, to craft an "anti-imperial literature of resistance."[24] In everything from the titles ascribed to God and the Lamb, to chapter 17's depiction of the goddess Roma as a prostitute, to the very word "empire," it intentionally mirrors specific elements of the Roman Empire, parodying them as "the absolute antithesis of 'the empire of God and his Messiah.'"[25]

Even more than Daniel, Revelation blurs the boundaries between human, more-than-human, and supernatural. The dramatic dual sign of a woman giving birth and a red dragon in chapter 12 offers a striking example.[26] Like Daniel, this chapter draws on older source material (including the book of Daniel itself) to present earthly struggles as expressions of supernatural forces. In it, the birth of a child identified with the messiah occasions a battle between the archangel Michael and the dragon, which is both satanic and, we learn in chapter 13, associated with empire. What is especially interesting here, though, are the ways more-than-human nature inserts itself into this supernatural narrative. When the dragon appears, it demonstrates its might by casting stars to the earth. When the woman flees after birthing the messiah, she is sheltered in the wilderness. As the conflict progresses, the woman grows eagles' wings; thus transformed—made more animal—she flees to her wilderness sanctuary. There, the earth itself comes to her aid, opening its mouth to swallow a torrent unleashed by the dragon. If, as some scholars have noted, one of Rome's sins in Revelation is its environmentally exploitative practices, the text imagines the earth fighting back.[27]

---

23 Collins, *The Apocalyptic Imagination*.

24 Stephen D. Moore, "The Revelation to John," in *A Postcolonial Commentary on the New Testament Writings*, ed. Fernando F. Segovia and R. S. Sugirtharajah (London and New York: T and T Clark, 2007), 441.

25 Moore, "The Revelation to John," 444.

26 For this discussion I am heavily indebted to an exceptionally well-researched student paper by the Rev. Rachel Eskite, submitted for "Environmental Ethics" in the fall semester of 2020, and I am grateful for her permission to use it here.

27 Barbara R. Rossing and Johan Buitendag, "Life in Its Fullness: Ecology, Eschatology and Ecodomy in a Time of Climate Change," *HTS Teologiese Studies/Theological Studies* 76, no. 1 (November 1, 2020): 4.

The land plays a crucial role in Revelation's restored creation as well. The vision of chapters 21 and 22, of a new heaven and earth, with a new Jerusalem, intentionally recalls the garden of Genesis 2. Here, as there, a river flows from God's throne with the water of life, and the tree of life stands on the bank (or, somewhat inexplicably, both banks) of the river, giving fruit year-round and leaves that are "for the healing of the nations"—that is, of the Gentiles. These images reference a similar vision in Ezekiel 47, where the river flows from the temple and into the sea, bringing life to the Dead Sea and nourishing the continually fruitful riparian trees. In Ezekiel, the river's life-giving power is explicitly tied to its origin in the sanctuary—that is, in the presence of God. In this idyllic vision, as elsewhere in the apocalyptic texts we have considered, more-than-human creation has clear agency in mediating God's restoration of creation. Here too, we see again that, like apocalyptic threat, apocalyptic hope also transcends the limitations of everyday discourse.

There is a tendency, particularly in some environmental theologies, to read Revelation's subversion of empire and proclamation of a new heaven and new earth as ethical exhortations. The promises of John's vision are taken as an invitation to a life transformed by the divine reign, typically characterized by harmony and broad community.[28] This is, in many ways, an understandable reaction against eschatological readings that take the supposed destruction of this world as license to neglect it. There are, however, exegetical and ethical reasons to be cautious here. It is true that, in contrast to other apocalyptic texts, Revelation's decisive act of deliverance has already taken place in Jesus. Nonetheless the context of the book is understood not as the time of fulfillment but rather the time of

---

28 See, for example, Henry G. Brinton, "Revelation 21:1–22:7," *Interpretation: A Journal of Bible & Theology* 70, no. 1 (January 2016): 84–86; Rossing and Buitendag, "Life in Its Fullness"; this is a different question from that of an ethical interpretation of Christian eschatology in general, as in J. Richard Middleton, *A New Heaven and a New Earth: Reclaiming Biblical Eschatology*, illustrated ed. (Grand Rapids, MI: Baker Academic, 2014).

suffering.[29] Moreover, while some apocalyptic literature has a clear hortatory function, the more obvious function of the genre seems to have been consolation in times of difficulty.[30] Finally, if Revelation is taken to have ethical implications, it is not at all clear that those implications would involve harmony and community. Rather, the dominant values are justice and judgment, and appropriate responses would seem mainly to be hope and perhaps martyrdom. As Collins puts it, "the ethics of Revelation are shaped by apocalyptic tradition rather than by Christian innovation." They reflect not primarily the teachings of Jesus, but rather the expectations of the genre.[31]

Here we do well to recall Demuth and Jenkins's wariness of apocalyptic strategies. Reading Revelation as an ethical text risks absolutizing environmental conflict and reinforcing already entrenched dualisms. In his postcolonial reading of Revelation, Stephen Moore argues that by intentionally using the language and trappings of the Roman Empire to portray God's reign, the book simply reinscribes the imperial structure with God at its center.[32] God's victory is a military victory over a lesser emperor, and the spoils are enjoyed only by God's subjects (22:14–15). The apocalyptic tradition of a divine reign that ends all human empires is not, finally, a repudiation of imperialism itself.

All of this is not to suggest that Revelation has no value for decolonial or antiracist environmental theology; far less is it to side with those who take the book as permission to neglect the present world. Rather, the point is that the book's value is not in its ethical implications, which are ambiguous at best, but in the rich imaginary resources it offers. Like other apocalyptic literature, and like other biblical traditions I will consider in this chapter, Revelation envisions a world of crossed boundaries—between human and more-than-human beings, between present and future, between earthly and heavenly realities. In this sense it is transgressive. Its words and

---

29 Collins, *The Apocalyptic Imagination*, chapter 9.
30 Collins, chapter 1.
31 Collins, chapter 9.
32 Moore, "The Revelation to John," 451–52.

images operate on several levels at once. Yes, it is a resource for hope; yet it also expresses fear, revulsion, irony, and violence. It speaks in many voices, precisely because no single perspective can comprehend either the crisis that motivates it or the hope that it proclaims.

II. TRANSGRESSIVE DESIRE

If the apocalyptic tradition seems at times to revel in the imperial structures it seeks to challenge, other transgressive texts in the Bible present strikingly different metaphors for a reimagined life of creation. The Song of Songs is a complex and enigmatic text whose implications for Christian environmentalism and environmental theology are rich and often overlooked. Where apocalypse emerges in response to the turmoil of political conflict, the Song reflects the intense urgency of desire. And like apocalyptic literature, the Song operates on multiple levels, such that no single interpretation can be said to capture its intent. A poetic account of two lovers—which never mentions God—has been interpreted as an allegory for the relationship between God and Israel, with direct correspondences drawn between the woman and the land, or for the relationship of God and the church. Historically it has been variously viewed as a drama involving two or three characters, a cycle of wedding songs, a single love poem, a collection of love poems, or a remnant of a fertility cult.[33] It is also the most allusive book in the Old Testament: like Daniel and Revelation, it adapts earlier phrases and texts to new contexts and new meanings.[34]

Throughout its text, the Song delights in blurring the boundaries between human and more-than-human, between character and setting, and between metaphor and reality. The lovers' bodies are compared with plants and trees and seemingly become them; they

---

33 John J. Collins, *Introduction to the Hebrew Bible: The Writings*, 3rd ed. (Minneapolis: Fortress Press, 2019), 93.

34 Davis, *Scripture, Culture, and Agriculture*, 170.

beckon one another to gardens and themselves become the gardens; the pleasures of landscape, food, and sex blend into one another.[35] As biblical scholar Mari Joerstad suggests, "its disregard for boundaries shows us that putting aside human specialness can be exquisite, that beyond our obsession with ourselves is a more satisfying way to live in the world."[36]

In various scenes, rich descriptions of a garden setting blend with metaphors for the lovers themselves. So, for example, chapter 2 begins by describing the woman as a lily and the man as an apple tree, then the man as a gazelle or stag and the woman as a dove. She then invites him to a lush vineyard, rich with descriptions of blossoms and fruits, and he is said to "graze" or "pasture his flock" among the lilies, alluding back to the description of the woman herself.

In some cases, this blending is helped by grammatical ambiguity. In chapter 4, a reference to a locked garden and a sealed spring may be a metaphor for the woman ("a locked garden is my sister, bride"), or may be a description of a place addressed to the woman ("a locked garden, O my sister, bride").[37] This ambiguity continues, as the woman invites the man to the garden to enjoy its fruits, leaving unanswered the question of whether the garden is the woman or the meeting-place. In a later scene (chapter 7), the man compares the woman variously to a date palm, a grapevine, and an apple tree, and her kisses to wine, before she invites him to the fields and vineyards, where she offers a promise of love, then immediately speaks again of fruits. In quick succession, "the pleasure of a spring landscape, the pleasure of sex, and the pleasure of fruits all blend into one; the woman is a bower, is a lover, is a host putting out delicacies for her guest."[38]

---

35 Mari Joerstad, *The Hebrew Bible and Environmental Ethics: Humans, Nonhumans, and the Living Landscape* (Cambridge and New York: Cambridge University Press, 2019), 188–91.

36 Joerstad, *The Hebrew Bible and Environmental Ethics*, 185.

37 Joerstad, 187.

38 Joerstad, 190.

Where apocalyptic literature transgresses the boundaries of human, more-than-human, and supernatural in the heat of cosmic battle, the Song transgresses those boundaries in the heat of desire. The lovers' desire for one another is so ardent that it draws in the rest of creation; or, seen another way, the bounty of creation is so generous that it encompasses the lovers' desire. And both are so gratuitous that they draw God and God's people into their symbolic world, and so enticing that inevitably the reader is immersed in the book's landscapes.[39] Scholars have pointed out that this expansive joining recalls what was lost in Genesis 2–3, and represents the healing of the ruptures that occurred there between man and woman, between human and the more-than-human world, and between humanity and God.[40] Joerstad suggests that the Song goes further than this: it imagines a world where the love and desire of each of these for the other is enough to overcome even the distinctions between them.[41]

Read in light of Anzaldúa's *nepantla* consciousness, the Song of Songs, like the apocalyptic texts we considered, responds to the exigency of a particular moment that resists everyday description—in this case, the urgency of human desire. It does so through a transgressive theology of creation; that is, one that crosses boundaries in ways that defy the epistemologies of colonialism. Together these texts overlay images of nature and the supernatural onto human struggles and passions, reading multiple layers of meaning simultaneously. Each of these books resists simplification: none of them can be said to mean just one thing. They incorporate ancient myths and themes into new contexts, where they take on new significance while retaining some of their original resonances. Moreover, all of them employ these strategies in service of subversive ends: Daniel and Revelation explicitly critique earthly empires, and the Song of Songs, with its exuberant desire, challenges the boundaries that divide creation.

---

39 Joerstad, 185.
40 Davis, *Scripture, Culture, and Agriculture*, 170.
41 Joerstad, *The Hebrew Bible and Environmental Ethics*, 192.

An anti-oppressive ecotheology will be characterized by greater attention to texts like these than has been the case with previous theologies. More than that, though, it will allow its imaginations to be shaped by them. It will embrace ambiguity and multivocality. It will stand within paradoxes, like those between the violent upheaval of apocalyptic literature and the intimate desire of the Song of Songs. It will attempt to speak, listen, and imagine on multiple levels of reality, as Anzaldúa does, not foreclosing the possibility, for example, that empires might be beasts, that trees might be lovers, that fruit might be sex, or that gardens might be active participants in our relationships.

All of this is admittedly still abstract. I have said something about what the sought-after theology might resemble, or how it might be approached. I have suggested some texts it might attend to, and how it might do so in relatively new ways. To describe more clearly what its content might be—that is, what it might say, or at least begin to say, about God and care for the environment, I turn to the most central example of a transgressive theme in Christian theology: the incarnation.

III. ALL THINGS HOLD TOGETHER

The incarnation is, of course, a defining doctrine—perhaps the defining doctrine—of Christian theology. It is also transgressive. It crosses boundaries. In the incarnation, God becomes human and yet remains God. An event of universal significance takes place in an irreducible particularity: a historical human being in first-century Palestine. As with apocalypse and the poetry of the Song, this transgressiveness responds to the urgency of a critical experience that resists ordinary description. In this case, that urgency is the early church's experience of the presence of God in the life of Jesus, and in the ongoing life of the church after his death.

According to theologian Niels Gregersen, "Since antiquity the Christian view that God's own Word or Logos (the eternal Son) assumed 'flesh' in Jesus of Nazareth has been seen as scandalous."[42] He notes that it was scandalous in three respects: materiality (that God should take on matter), suffering (that God should be "involved in the messy lives of human sinners and victims"), and uniqueness (that God would identify in a unique way with this particular human being). "All three," he reflects, "seem to apply to the Christian belief in the Son of God being born of a woman in a dirty manger, drinking and eating with unclean people and dying on a cross together with criminals."[43] In the fourth century, the church father Gregory of Nyssa mused that when Christians proclaim that "the word was made flesh" (John 1:15), that "the light shined in the darkness" (John 1:5), and that "life tasted death" (Heb 2:9), they are witnessing to a God whose power is manifested "by means external to [God's] own nature."[44] Reflecting on Gregory, John Behr points out that in crossing the boundary between divine and human, between creator and creature, God destabilizes that boundary: "death is destroyed by death, and so death becomes the means of life; light shines in the darkness, transforming the darkness into light; the Word was manifest in flesh, and so makes the flesh Word."[45] It is this transgressive doctrine that is, in St. Paul's words, "a stumbling block" and "foolishness" (1 Cor 1:23): the incarnation defies our attempts to understand it in simple terms or straightforward categories.

This boundary-crossing character of the incarnation has been generative for Christian environmental theology. That God chooses to unite Godself with a human body is typically taken to mean that God is deeply invested in the interests and suffering of the world of flesh and matter. Environmental theologians rightly point out that this has profound implications for our care for God's creation. As

---

42 Niels Henrik Gregersen, "Introduction," in *Incarnation: On the Scope and Depth of Christology*, ed. Niels Henrik Gregersen (Minneapolis: Fortress Press, 2015), 3–4.

43 Gregersen, "Introduction," 4.

44 Quoted in John Behr, "Saint Athanasius on 'Incarnation,'" in Gregersen, *Incarnation*, 80.

45 Behr, "Saint Athanasius on 'Incarnation,'" 80–81.

Celia Deane-Drummond writes, "the point is that if Christ is in some way identified with the earth, then Christians have an added reason to care for that earth, quite apart from belief in God as Creator."[46]

One of the most influential accounts of this view of the incarnation is ecofeminist theologian Sallie McFague's book *The Body of God*. In this seminal text, McFague argues for an "organic model" of theology that views the material universe, with its evolutionary dynamism and infinite relations, as God's body.[47] This is a panentheist theology: God is in all finite things, nothing exists apart from God, yet the reality of God is not exhausted by finite reality.[48] McFague's model envisions the spirit of God as what gives life to the body, to every individual creaturely body, and to the whole of the universe.

In this theological context, what is essential about the incarnation is that God became flesh and lived among us as a human being. Both "the concrete physical availability of God's presence" and "the likeness to ourselves, a human being" are crucial.[49] The story of Jesus of Nazareth further specifies the meaning of the incarnation by suggesting a trajectory for the world that is moral or teleological—that is, driven toward a purpose or goal. "From the paradigmatic story of Jesus we will propose that the direction of creation is toward inclusive love for all, especially the oppressed, the outcast, the vulnerable."[50] Thus while Jesus is, for McFague, one of many possible paradigmatic expressions of the presence of God in the universe, this particular embodiment is distinctive in its focus on those humans and nonhumans who are oppressed and suffering.

Environmental theologies in general have taken a broadly similar approach to the incarnation to that of McFague: that in becoming

---

46 Celia Deane-Drummond, *A Primer in Ecotheology: Theology for a Fragile Earth*, Cascade Companions 37 (Eugene, OR: Cascade Books, 2017), chapter 5.

47 Sallie McFague, *The Body of God: An Ecological Theology* (Minneapolis: Fortress Press, 1993).

48 McFague, *The Body of God*, 149.

49 McFague, 160.

50 McFague, 160.

flesh in Jesus, God demonstrates a special concern for or solidarity with the created world. More recently this view has been articulated and more fully developed with the idea of a "deep incarnation."[51] As described by Niels Gregersen, the theologian who first coined the term, deep incarnation is the view that "the Logos of God (the eternal Son) 'became flesh' in Jesus, assumed a particular body and mind in him, and hereby also conjoined the material, living, and mental conditions of being a creature in any epoch."[52] The human flesh that God assumed was "a complex unit of minerals and fluids, an item in the carbon, oxygen, and nitrogen cycles, a moment in the biological evolution of this planet."[53] Because human matter is part of the history of the cosmos, God enters into solidarity not only with human life but with "the whole biophysical world of which human beings are a part."[54] Deep incarnation makes McFague's organic model more specific, showing how the incarnation of God in Jesus Christ really does unite God with all flesh, with "flesh" understood as broadly, but also as concretely, as possible.

This view similarly extends the reach of the traditional notion of the corporate body of Christ. New Testament language that refers to the church as the body of Christ seems to conceive of the risen Christ as really present—and thus the incarnation as in some sense continued—in the gathered community.[55] The lens of deep incarnation, with its attention to the way all bodies are interdependent and constituted by ecological relationship, can further develop this claim by arguing that the community, as physically embodied, does participate in the concrete reality that also made up Jesus's body. It can also thereby extend the idea of Christ's body to include the

---

51 Niels Henrik Gregersen, "The Cross of Christ in an Evolutionary World," *Dialog: A Journal of Theology* 40, no. 3 (September 2001): 192.

52 Gregersen, "Introduction," 7.

53 Elizabeth A. Johnson, "Jesus and the Cosmos," in Gregersen, *Incarnation*, 138.

54 Johnson, "Jesus and the Cosmos," 140.

55 Christopher Southgate, "Depth, Sign and Destiny," in Gregersen, *Incarnation*, 216.

whole range of ecological relationships in which Christ's corporate body is implicated.[56]

Yet, as biblical scholar Richard Bauckham insists, this seemingly unorthodox view is wholly consistent with the biblical view that God's redemption extends to all creation.[57] Indeed, this view may help interpret passages that describe a "cosmic Christ," as in 1 Colossians: "He is the image of the invisible God, the firstborn of all creation; ... in him all things hold together ... and through him God was pleased to reconcile to himself all things, whether on earth or in heaven, by making peace through the blood of his cross" (vv. 15, 17, 20). These cosmic Christ passages suggest that the one who became incarnate in Jesus of Nazareth is the same one who was present at creation and continues to sustain the world.[58] Moreover, in these passages, Christ's redemption of creation seems not to be mediated through human salvation but rather more directly.

Some theologians of the early church held a worldview that understood humans to share somehow in the essence of all other creatures—stones, trees, animals, and angels.[59] Maximus the Confessor, an influential theologian in the sixth and seventh centuries in the Byzantine Empire, developed an intricate Christology where Christ, because he is human, can bring all creation within the reach of salvation. Maximus believed there were multiple fundamental divisions within reality, but that human beings were able, in their ascent toward union with God, to unite the two poles of each division; indeed, this was their role in creation.[60] Since they had failed to perform this role, Christ became incarnate as a human being to fulfil it. Within Maximus's worldview, Christ was able to bring the

---

56 Southgate, "Depth, Sign and Destiny," 219; Niels Henrik Gregersen, "The Extended Body of Christ," in Gregersen, *Incarnation*, 242.

57 Richard Bauckham, "The Incarnation and the Cosmic Christ," in Gregersen, *Incarnation*, 35.

58 Bauckham, 35.

59 Bauckham, 37–39.

60 Bauckham, 39.

whole creation into union with God precisely because human beings, as human beings, are already connected to all that exists.

To the extent that his worldview might plausibly be compared to contemporary ecological worldviews, Maximus provides a helpful precedent for deep incarnation, and intriguing possibilities for our consideration of transgressive themes for a decolonial environmental theology. If, instead of Maximus's intricate system of dualisms, we begin from an understanding of ecological interrelatedness, we can affirm his belief that by becoming a creature among other creatures—that is to say, a biological being, "made out of stardust and earth"[61]—Christ is able to unify all creation with himself, and thus with God. We may or may not wish to preserve his insistence on humanity's uniqueness in this ability to unite the various categories. We can nonetheless affirm the traditional doctrine that Christ accomplishes this union in a unique way, that God is present to creation in a unique way as the particular human being Jesus of Nazareth.[62] Because Jesus was a human being, a participant in ecological relationships as all human beings are, God's incarnation as Jesus can be cosmic in scope; this does not necessarily mean, however, that all human beings, by virtue of their ecological relationships, are capable of this act of unification. Recall that for Maximus, Jesus fulfills this role because human beings fail to do so. As theologian and scientist Arthur Peacocke puts it, in a contemporary variation on Maximus's Christology, "the significance and potentiality of all levels of creation may be said to have been unfolded in Jesus the Christ."[63]

What Maximus adds to the ecological Christology of deep incarnation, though, and what makes his thought particularly intriguing for the theology I am developing, is the sense of boundaries being crossed. For Maximus, it is because humankind is capable of bridging the division, for example, between what is perceived by the mind and what is perceived by the senses, that the human being Jesus

---

61 Gregersen, "Introduction," 7.
62 Cf. Bauckham, "The Incarnation and the Cosmic Christ," 55.
63 Quoted in Bauckham, 41.

can redeem creation. In other words, the incarnation crosses the boundaries within creation and between creation and God. The fact that Maximus's dualistic worldview has been replaced by one of ecological interrelatedness does not negate this transgressive character; to the contrary, it simply confirms that humans, as ecological beings, always already straddle the boundaries we would construct around ourselves. In our bodies, we incorporate the human and nonhuman, the organic and inorganic, the animate and inanimate. We unite our evolutionary past and planetary future. The incarnation places God in the midst of this messy material reality.

Perhaps the most fundamental boundary transgressed by the incarnation is that between immanence and transcendence. Traditionally, theology has held that God is transcendent, that is, apart from or beyond creation. This transcendence has often been viewed in tension with affirmation of God's immanence, God's presence and activity within creation. The incarnation is not the only expression of God's immanence, but it is a unique and paradigmatic one. For in the incarnation, the transcendent God enters creation precisely as God, as a particular human being in a particular time.

There are many views on the precise relation between the incarnation and other expressions of God's immanence more generally in creation, even among those theologies being considered here. For some (such as McFague), the incarnation is a paradigmatic or culminating moment in an ongoing relationship of God's presence in creation; for others (such as Bauckham), God is present as Christ in a way that is quite distinct from God's presence in the rest of creation. Those differences notwithstanding, whatever else deep incarnation may mean for God's immanence, it entails that God is present in and through the ecological relationships that constitute every creature and all creation. When God assumes human personhood, God assumes life in ecological community, and indeed, life as an ecological community. Thus God's immanence is to be found in such community, in the boundary-transgressing relationships that unite all creatures and all creation.

One innovative approach to God's transcendence and immanence can help us see the implications of this for Christian environmentalism and ecotheology. In *The Touch of Transcendence*, Mayra Rivera proposes a postcolonial theology of God's transcendence.[64] Rivera is concerned with an overemphasis on God's transcendence, and especially with theologies that implicitly conceive that transcendence in terms of physical space.[65] This implicit understanding is often accompanied by a sense that God's primary mode of engagement with creation is through a form of power that is controlling and distant, which in turn gives rise to a series of dualisms that serve to separate and oppress certain types of persons. Thus if God's transcendence is associated with immateriality, rationality, and autonomy (and, not coincidentally, often with the male gender), God's immanence is associated with materiality, sensibility, and dependence (and often the female gender), and this latter set of categories is understood to be inferior.[66]

In response to this understanding of transcendence in terms of spatial distance, Rivera draws on several postmodern and postcolonial philosophers and theologians—principally Emmanuel Levinas, Enrique Dussel, Luce Irigaray, and Gayatri Spivak—to suggest a conception of God's transcendence that is immersed in the world, in creaturely relationship. Rivera argues that in every encounter between human beings, indeed between any bodies, there is something that eludes our grasp. In every "Other" that I encounter, no matter how intimately, there is an irreducible part of that Other that is inaccessible to me.[67] This is the transcendence of the Other, and it is, for Rivera, an expression of God's transcendence within the world. This transcendence, she says, "flows through reality as the sap through the branches of a tree."[68]

---

64 Mayra Rivera, *The Touch of Transcendence: A Postcolonial Theology of God* (Louisville, KY: Westminster John Knox Press, 2007).
65 Rivera, *The Touch of Transcendence*, 3–4.
66 Rivera, 6.
67 Rivera, 77, 81–82.
68 Rivera, 53.

Crucially, this transcendence of the Other is not located in their individuality, their separation from me and all others, but rather in their relationality. Because every person, every self, exists as a web of relationships—with other human beings, with the more-than-human world, and with God—their being extends out infinitely, and it is this infinite relationality that is irreducible, exceeding the grasp of any one individual encounter. Moreover, because these relational beings are necessarily embodied, so too is this transcendence an embodied, incarnate transcendence.[69] Here Rivera means incarnation both generally, as the insistence that the Others we encounter are always necessarily enfleshed and embodied, and also with reference to Christ's incarnation, as the revelation that the transcendent God does indeed will to be present in these embodied relationships.[70] And this relational transcendence clearly extends to the ecological relationships that constitute us as bodies. In language that echoes Maximus, she insists, "as mediators of the becoming of the cosmos, human beings meet the transcendence . . . of the whole creation."[71] Later, she adds, "interhuman transcendence takes place in and contributes to cosmic co-creation. The interhuman, the cosmic, and the social converge."[72]

This encounter with the transcendence of the Other, and in them, God's transcendence, has ethical implications. We are accountable to the Other; their irreducibility imposes responsibilities on us. Principally, these responsibilities involve recognizing and respecting that transcendence. In other words, the encounter with the Other calls us to see them as transcendent, as one whose true nature exceeds our grasp—as something more than an object that I define with reference to myself.[73] This work involves deconstructing the systems that reduce the Other to an object or category. In the words of liberation theologian Roberto Goizueta, "in an era dominated . . .

---

69 Rivera, 93.
70 Rivera, 92–93.
71 Rivera, 93.
72 Rivera, 129.
73 Rivera, 60–61.

by capitalist economic monopolies, the defense of human and divine transcendence is no longer a mere option; it is the principal and most urgent imperative."[74] This work further requires examining and rejecting the historical discourses of colonialism and imperialism that construct difference as if it were natural and objective.[75] All of this, of course, includes the economic, political, and epistemological systems through which whiteness is constructed and maintained, as described in Chapter 3.

The relationality that constitutes the beings in these encounters also extends through time. In our relational, embodied selves, we incorporate the injuries of the past and project possibilities into the future. Accordingly, this ethical task of deconstruction must be able to extend into the past and future.[76] Rivera's theology of transcendence does this by acknowledging that the relationships of which we are made include both past and future in the present. It recognizes the ways our social systems are products—"sedimentations"—of past social relations, and the ways they produce and shape future possibilities. This is especially crucial for an ecological theology that incorporates this sense of relational transcendence. Only by spanning the boundary between past, present, and future, by bringing past events and future possibilities into the encounters of the present, can we adequately address past ecological harms (historical fossil fuel emissions, for example) that threaten future generations.

In its thoroughly relational anthropology and cosmology, its insistence that God's transcendence occurs in incarnate encounters between beings who are socially and ecologically embedded in relationship, Rivera's theology of transcendence further develops the possibilities raised by deep incarnation. More specifically, she describes the ethical implications of this sense of God's profound identification with embodied reality. She explains why this divine presence calls forth an ethical response: because it calls our attention

---

74 Quoted in Rivera, 69.
75 Rivera, 103.
76 Rivera, 119.

to the irreducibility of human and more-than-human Others, that aspect of their being that can never be grasped or contained. While she does not focus on Christ's incarnation, it is the theological foundation for her affirmation of the transcendent God's presence within creation. In the radically transgressive doctrine of the incarnation, which crosses so many boundaries, we find confirmation that to exist in creation is necessarily to exist across boundaries. And it is precisely in this boundary-crossing relationality that God chooses to be present to God's creation.

IV. CONCLUSION: THE ECO-POLITICAL BODY OF CHRIST

This chapter began where the previous chapter ended: with Gloria Anzaldúa's invocation of *nepantla* consciousness, a way of thinking across boundaries that might be capable of resisting the narrow epistemologies of colonialism I have described. I have suggested three theological themes that share this boundary-crossing, or transgressive, character: the multilayered images of apocalyptic literature, the playful fluidity of the Song of Songs, and the transgressive doctrine of the incarnation, especially as developed by advocates of deep incarnation. These disparate themes begin to come together in Rivera's theology of transcendence. The recognition that our deep ecological relatedness is an expression of God's transcendence in the world elicits in us a sense of straddling boundaries. Precisely as human beings, bodies embedded in networks of other bodies across time and space, we are involved in a divine life that reaches across multiple realities and yet immerses itself in our world, in all times and places, but especially as one specific body in first-century Palestine.

Like the themes considered here, anti-oppressive ecotheology sprouts from the soil of urgency: an existential moment that resists mundane discourse and destabilizes conventional boundaries. What seems to be a world-ending crisis turns out, in fact, to be just that, only in a different sense. The world created by our categories, framed by boundaries, comes apart, unveiling the deep transgressive relations that link us to one another and to more-than-human others, to past and future, by deconstructing the illusions of individualism, whiteness, colonialism, and others that obscure the reality of those relations.

This ecotheology thus learns how to respond to this moment of existential threat from boundary-crossing imaginations like those found in Daniel, Revelation, and the Song of Songs, among other places. It follows Anzaldúa's resistance to colonial ways of knowing, refusing to shut down these rich imaginary landscapes by restricting them to one level of meaning. Trees may be simultaneously a meeting place for lovers, metaphors for those same lovers, and, through ecological relationship, part of what constitutes those lovers in their encounter. Empires or systems may be diabolical, not only metaphorically but in reality, in the ways they oppose the relational transcendence through which God is present in creation. Battle may be an apt descriptor for this opposition, even as loving desire may be what most characterizes that embodied transcendence. And, like the Crow people in Willis Jenkins's example, we may find in apocalypse and transcendence hopeful visions that are as inconceivable as they are necessary.

As they reestablish embodied-transcendent connections across the boundaries of whiteness, apocalypse, desire, and incarnation thus give rise to a collective ecological body. It is a body that works toward deconstruction, and toward the construction of systems and communities that recognize and respect that relational transcendence. As theologian Catherine Keller describes it in her provocative *Political Theology of the Earth*, "the 'new creation' does not signify, even in the biblical apocalypse, a final solution but the dis/closure of the participatory collective of the creation in its interspecies, intra-planetary agency."[77] Keller begins her argument by reflecting on 1 Corinthians 7:29: "The appointed time is short." The sense here is not

---

77 Catherine Keller, *Political Theology of the Earth: Our Planetary Emergency and the Struggle for a New Public* (New York: Columbia University Press, 2018), 115.

of a ticking clock but of a contracted and intensified time, a decisive moment in which to act; and an imminent end, not of the world but of its present order.[78] And so, again, consideration of the end times unveils deep bonds of creaturely dependence—what she calls "intercarnation"—hidden by the dominant systems.[79] This unveiling creates the potential for new collectives, "the gathering of a public across critical difference," and thus it is ultimately political, in the broad sense of the formation of a *polis*, a public.[80]

With respect to the characteristics laid out in the previous chapter for a decolonial environmental theology, the theology I have described here is pluralist, public, and pragmatic. More specifically, its pluralism is reflected in the engagement with Anzaldúa's *nepantla*: it embraces multiple, diverse, and even apparently contradictory ways of knowing. Yet as I also insisted, this pluralism is a grounded pluralism; these ways of knowing are united by embodied connections to one another and to the earth, to our places. It is public, and more precisely counterpublic, in its formation of collectives that struggle against systems of division and domination. These two characteristics, its publicness and its pluralism, create the potential for the third characteristic, pragmatism. Recall that pragmatist approaches originate not in preconceived ideas but in the lived moral experiences of communities. How this approach might pragmatically engage with and learn from the moral agency of communities will become clearer in the next chapter. In this chapter, though, I have been more concerned with the prophetic character of the pragmatic approach I described: that is, how we might develop imaginative resources that take us outside conventional ways of thought and allow us to challenge the status quo.

The collective body of Christ affirmed by the New Testament therefore turns out, in this anti-oppressive ecotheology, to be an ecological and political body. It is a community formed across boundaries,

---

78 Keller, *Political Theology of the Earth*, 4–5.
79 Keller, 99.
80 Keller, 164.

through deep ecological relationships, in opposition to the systems and ways of knowing that would reinforce those boundaries and deny those relationships. The task of forming this eco-political body of Christ—of first imagining and then gathering an ecological public across boundaries of race, gender, species, animacy—is the fundamental challenge for an anti-oppressive Christian environmentalism. It is to the practical and ethical aspects of this challenge that I turn in the final chapter.

CHAPTER 5

The Eco-Political Body of Christ

The three sisters—corn, beans, and squash—spread out in various forms across multiple tables set beneath maple trees. Cornbread, bean salad, bean cakes, chili, squash casserole, and soup embrace one another on the tables, just as their respective plants held and supported one another in the garden. Before eating, the diners head to the garden to gather more ears of corn, green beans, and squash blossoms.

This is how Robin Wall Kimmerer describes her annual summer Three Sisters potluck.[1] She explains how for millennia, native people have recognized and depended on the complex, even miraculous mutualisms of these three crops. Corn grows fast and tall, emerging in the summer and creating a strong stalk. As the bean plant emerges, it first grows low along the ground before sending out a vine that traces a circle in the air, seeking out a vertical support. Finding the cornstalk, it holds on and grows upward while its roots transform nitrogen into a form useful to the other plants. Squash emerges last, its broad leaves and bristly vines offering its sisters protection from insects and other plants and holding in moisture. This botanical reciprocity is paralleled by nutritional reciprocity: corn provides carbohydrates, beans provide protein, and squash provides important

---

1 Kimmerer, *Braiding Sweetgrass*, 137.

vitamins. This sophistication was, of course, totally lost on the colonists, who labeled the Native Americans as savages and considered their agricultural practices ignorant.

In Kimmerer's rich prose, though, the biological relationships become loving social relationships, relationships mirrored in the human and interspecies relationships expressed in the feast. The plants speak to each other and to human beings in their growth, their transformation of sunlight and water into food energy, their connections to one another.[2] And at the feast, these connections spread out like the "three-dimensional sprawl of abundance" of the sisters. There, all are kin: eaters and planters; corn, beans, and squash; plants and insects; soil, air, and water.

I. RADICAL IMAGINATION AND ACTION

The previous chapter showed how the theological themes of apocalypse, desire, and incarnation can together engender an imagination of Christ's body as an eco-political body. I suggested that decolonizing Christian environmentalism requires us to imagine and then gather an ecological public that transcends—or transgresses—the boundaries created by whiteness. In other words, I am arguing that we need to find ways of conceiving ecological community that destabilizes our conceptions of ourselves as autonomous and independent; that enacts our radical connections with one another across race and ethnic identity, gender, sexuality, and even species; and that encompasses not only different ways of valuing but deeply divergent ways of knowing.

Kimmerer's poignant reflection, which resembles nothing so much as an ecological and gustatory vision of the eschatological banquet, offers a glimpse of such an ecological community. The feast she describes embraces human and more-than-human in reciprocal community; they share gifts and stories, and listen and learn from

---

2 Kimmerer, 129.

one another. For Kimmerer, the Three Sisters represent an ethical and epistemological pluralism, as well—a possible reciprocity of Western science with Indigenous knowledge and ethics. She imagines the corn, which gives structure to the partnership, as traditional ecological knowledge. The "curious bean" twining its way up the corn is Western science. The squash, which provides protection for the other two, is an ethical vision of coexistence and mutual flourishing. In this way, Kimmerer's potluck is an image of an ecological community that crosses social and ideological boundaries. In this it is also political: the meal is a work of radical imagination of new ways of being together, new publics that take our mutual interdependence profoundly seriously.

This is a daunting, perhaps impossible, imaginative task. In Anzaldúa's words, "it takes energy and courage, to name ourselves and grow beyond cultural and self-imposed boundaries."[3] Mari Joerstad, whose interpretation of the Song of Songs informed the previous chapter, is clear on the difficulty of inhabiting such a worldview. "Despite my best intentions," she laments, "I cannot share in the experience of living in a world full of persons, only some of whom are human. . . . The West has made a practice of assuming that our own concepts, our science, objectivity, and rationality, are better and more enlightened than those of other peoples."[4] She is correct, of course, that most of us formed in the dominant culture of the West are unable truly to inhabit the seemingly more alive, more mutualistic worldview of the Song of Songs, or the mythic cosmology of apocalyptic literature. At the same time, for contemporary Christians, these are our texts, too; their images and language are part of our imaginative vocabulary, even if we have shied away from some of their implications.

We might even have some experience with this kind of imagination. As children, we intuitively attribute agency and intention to animals and plants; we must be conditioned to view creation as

---

3 Anzaldúa, *Light in the Dark*, 93.
4 Joerstad, *The Hebrew Bible and Environmental Ethics*, 47.

inanimate and inert. Even then, there are moments when we find this much-prized objectivity slipping, when we find ourselves inadvertently seeing a friendly animal or even a familiar tree as kin, as a fellow person. We are constantly reminded of the dangers of anthropomorphism, of attributing human characteristics to nonhuman creatures. There are certainly reasons to be wary of such a move in the wrong contexts; yet perhaps this risk can represent an opportunity to cultivate new imaginations.

Kimmerer powerfully describes how learning "the grammar of animacy" changed her view of the world. Learning her ancestral language of Potawatomi as an adult, she was struck by how its vocabulary and syntax seem to bring the world to life. Potawatomi has proportionally far more verbs than English, many for ideas that English communicates as nouns. Kimmerer relates the moment when she realized the implications of this fact: "To be a hill, to be a sandy beach, to be a Saturday, all are possible verbs in a world where everything is alive. Water, land, and even a day, the language a mirror for seeing the animacy of the world, the life that pulses through all things, through pies and nuthatches and mushrooms."[5] Similarly, many things that in English would be inanimate, in Potawatomi are animate beings: "In Potawatomi 101, rocks are animate, as are mountains and water and fire and places." "Imagine," she muses, "walking through a richly inhabited world of Birch people, Bear people, Rock people, beings we think of and therefore speak of as persons worthy of our respect, of inclusion in a peopled world."[6] Joerstad may be correct that such experiences of radical imagination do not come easily, yet they are not completely unfamiliar or inaccessible to us. As she reflects, "I would like to know what it is like to talk to a tree or what a stone might say to me. . . . This project is an exercise in waiting, in listening to others who have listened to the world."[7]

---

5 Kimmerer, *Braiding Sweetgrass*, 55.

6 Kimmerer, 56.

7 Joerstad, *The Hebrew Bible and Environmental Ethics*, 47.

Daunting though the imaginative task may be, it may be far less challenging than the actual practices of forming such reconciled ecological community. As I have noted repeatedly, an anti-oppressive environmental theology requires more than shifting ideologies. It demands real, practical changes, attempting to remove the material political, economic, and social barriers that prevent us from being reconciled to one another. The construction of whiteness, through racism and settler-colonialism, creates real debts, including environmental debts, that must be confronted in any attempt to forge ecological community. This must be challenging, because it cannot be done without relinquishing the power and privilege that have been secured through the disempowerment and exclusion of people of color and Indigenous people.

In this chapter, I suggest the practices and skills needed to imagine and gather ecological community beyond whiteness: an ecological community that transgresses the divisions and boundaries constructed by imaginations of whiteness. First, I argue that liturgy develops the skills necessary to shift worldviews and imagine such possibilities. I then consider suggestive examples of the formation of these kinds of counter-publics in community organizations. Finally, I apply the discourse and practice of reparations to environmental injustices, drawing on important contemporary discussions of reparations as "worldmaking."

II. TRANSFORMING LITURGY

One thing that becomes apparent with Kimmerer's account of learning Potawatomi is that imaginative shifts involve more than simply thinking differently. They require practice: they must be put into action and habituated. Kimmerer's changing perspective came after months of frustrating practice learning the skill of a new language. She recounts placing Post-it Notes all over her house, and squeezing in lessons and practice over lunch and in the evenings.[8]

---

8 Kimmerer, *Braiding Sweetgrass*, 52.

She established rituals, like responding out loud to the Potawatomi query posted on her back door asking where she was going. She understood the animacy of the language only as she practiced the skill of speaking.

Undoing the whiteness of environmental theology, conceiving new imaginations of reconciled ecological community, demands practice. As Christopher Carter insists, "the pervasive nature of coloniality has become a habit, a disposition from which we make sense of our everyday encounters and justify the exponential social, educational, and economic inequality within our society . . . *Coloniality often feels normal.* Undoing the habit of colonial thinking requires us to develop new habits. . . ."[9] Because coloniality and whiteness are so deeply rooted in our habits of thinking and acting, through generations of practice, challenging and uprooting that whiteness similarly takes practice, the formation of new habits. It is an effort that must be embodied in actions and repeated over time. Practices that express a transformed vision of community can shape imaginations and make possible new, previously unimagined possibilities. For Christian theology, of course, this is precisely what liturgy is and does.

"Liturgy shapes the imaginations and dispositions of agents by inducting them into the interior and exterior habits of love," says Willis Jenkins.[10] Etymologically, *leitourgia* necessarily involves the *laos*, the people or public. As I argued in the previous chapter, our task is to understand the public expansively, to include all the more-than-human participants in the body of Christ. Echoing the deep incarnation theme, Alexander Schmemann insists that "it is only because the Church's *leitourgia* is always cosmic, i.e. assumes into Christ all creation, and is always historical, i.e. assumes into Christ all time, that it can therefore become eschatological, i.e., make us true participants of the Kingdom to come."[11] In this cosmic formulation, liturgy can be the ongoing imaginative practice of gathering

---

9 Carter, *The Spirit of Soul Food*, 125 (italics in original).
10 Jenkins, *The Future of Ethics*, 308.
11 Cited in Jenkins, 313.

a community across intra- and inter-species boundaries and across generations.

Argentinian liberation philosopher Enrique Dussel emphasizes how liturgy exemplifies the entanglement of human beings' encounter with God in the midst of the complexity of creation. The bread and wine of Eucharist, for example, "is *at the same time* the 'substance of the Eucharistic offering' and the 'fruit of common labor, exchanged among those who produce it.'"[12] To this we might add that this eucharistic offering gathers up the work of wheat and vine to convert soil, air, water, and sunlight into carbohydrates; and, beyond those, the lives of fungi, insects, and worms; and cycles of nutrients, minerals, and water. Just like the Three Sisters potluck, the eucharistic feast ramifies in all directions, incorporating—that is, embodying—in one moment the relations between God and creation and among all human and more-than-human creatures. Dussel describes it as economic, in that it represents the practices of economic exchange; in this sense, it is also political, in that it encompasses the systems and dynamics that govern our various relationships.

Of course, Eucharist, like liturgy more broadly, also gathers community across generations. Communities receive liturgical traditions from their ancestors, and they sustain and nurture them for future generations of worshippers. Where the Anthropocene epoch and climate change represent a catastrophic failure to value future generations—what some have provocatively called "child sacrifice"—liturgical tradition offers a powerful counter-imagination.[13] "The act of liturgy," argues Jenkins, "is itself a transgenerational ethic, performing the communion of saints with inherited forms of interruption and anticipation." Liturgy brings the past into the present, transforming how we might imagine the future.

Liturgy can also transform the past. At the center of eucharistic theology is the notion of *anamnesis*, an act of remembering rooted in Jesus's command at the last supper to "do this in memory of

---

12 Cited in Rivera, *The Touch of Transcendence*, 71 (italics in original).
13 Jenkins, *The Future of Ethics*, 306.

me." For womanist theologian M. Shawn Copeland, this eucharistic remembering casts a clear-eyed gaze to the "dead, exploited, despised victims of history," telling the difficult truths of history as the beginning of a real, concrete solidarity.[14] Eucharist links the bodily suffering of these victims, especially women of color, to Christ's own suffering body and to his collective body, the church, drawing it to embrace the despised and marginalized bodies of our own time. In this way, Eucharist is a habit, an ongoing "practice of cognitive and bodily commitments" that "forms our social imagination, transvalues our values, and transforms the meaning of our being human, of embodying Christ."[15] If the goal for environmental theology and Christian environmentalism is to gather a new political-ecological community that transcends social and temporal boundaries, Eucharist might represent an especially apt practice for learning and habituating the skill of imagining such a community.

Unfortunately, most liturgy fails to cultivate these skills. Indeed, many of our liturgies fail to gather community across the street, much less across the boundaries forged by racism and colonialism. Recall Traci West's critiques, discussed in Chapter 2, of the subtle ways liturgy in predominantly white worship communities reinforces assumptions of whiteness.[16] Even in seemingly well-intentioned efforts at inclusiveness and multiculturalism, communities may speak from an assumed white identity, or may appeal to generalities that erase, rather than embrace, particular groups' experiences of marginalization. For predominantly white churches to enact liturgies that gather communities across social and ecological boundaries will require more radical reorientations and explicit attention to power. "To destabilize patterns of social dominance" in liturgy, says West, "will mean deliberately making choices that risk diminishing one's access to certain benefits of social privilege or status."[17] As

---

14 M. Shawn Copeland, *Enfleshing Freedom: Body, Race, and Being* (Minneapolis: Fortress Press, 2009), 100.

15 Copeland, *Enfleshing Freedom*, 127.

16 West, *Disruptive Christian Ethics*, 124–28.

17 West, 138.

one possible example of such liberative liturgy, she suggests a "God asks who is supposed to dispose of your trash" week during Advent, where households could learn about the "racial/ethnic and economic 'geography' of trash and toxic waste disposal," and could incorporate trash and environmental justice into Sunday worship.[18]

For his part, Jenkins turns to two ancient traditions, "the liturgy of the poor" and "cosmic liturgy," to urge the church toward more radically inclusive forms of worship.[19] The first practice, liturgy of the poor, recognizes that "feeding the poor is sacramental, because . . . Christ comes in the body of the hungry and suffering."[20] Acts of charity like feeding ministries are here incorporated into the fabric of the liturgy as an expression of the Eucharist, the moment of encounter with the incarnate God in the world, in real bodies before us. This ancient practice might help form antiracist and decolonial imaginations in the church not because the poor are here identified with communities of color but because in it we might learn to see differently. In such a liturgy, we might learn and practice the skill of transgressing the divisions of constructed identities, including those built on whiteness and colonialism, and encountering one another in the "relational transcendence" discussed in Chapter 4. We might practice the skills needed to imagine a new kind of eco-political body.

Cosmic liturgy extends this practice even further, recognizing with Schmemann above how liturgy encompasses all creation. Speaking from the perspective of deep incarnation described in the last chapter, Elizabeth Johnson revels in the way the Roman Catholic liturgy of Easter expresses this breadth:

> [The liturgy] symbolizes [cosmic resurrection] with cosmic and earthy symbols of light and dark, new fire, flowers and greens, water and oil, bread and wine. The thrilling *Exsultet*, sung only once a year on this night, shouts, "Exult, all creation, around God's throne! Jesus Christ our king is risen!" The proclamation continues:

---

18 West, 139–40.
19 Jenkins, *The Future of Ethics*, 312.
20 Jenkins, 312.

Rejoice, O earth, in shining splendor

radiant in the brightness of your king!

Christ has conquered! Glory fills you!

Darkness vanishes forever![21]

Such resources are certainly present in the tradition. Yet just as our worship usually fails to be adequately inclusive of other humans, so too are most of our liturgies what Jenkins calls "monoculture liturgies," "focused on a God–human dyad that seems naked of creation."[22] He suggests that churches exercise liturgical creativity and learn from Indigenous rituals to craft worship that includes more-than-human creation. Of course, such learning needs to be paired with real action toward material reparations, as I will describe below, if it is to avoid further settler-colonialist exploitation.

The *podong* rite of the Igorot people of the mountain region of the Philippines may be an example of just such Indigenous liturgical creativity with eco-political implications. Ferdinand Anno describes this practice of planting reed sticks in the ground as a part of a larger ritual.[23] Functionally, the *podong* sticks indicate that a ritual act is being performed, and proclaim a time of rest for the people and the land. Beyond this, however, the sticks represent a passageway through which ancestral spirits can join with the living: "It is this communion of the living, the ancestral spirits, the earth, and all that dwell therein . . . that calls on people and every living being to observe solemnity."[24] In the context of struggles over ancestral lands, such as the struggle against large-scale open-pit

---

21 Johnson, "Jesus and the Cosmos," 150.

22 Jenkins, *The Future of Ethics*, 313.

23 Ferdinand Anno, "On Earth as in Heaven: The Earth in the Podong Leitourgia of the Post-Human Commune," in *Decolonizing Ecotheology: Indigenous and Subaltern Challenges*, ed. S. Lily Mendoza and George Zachariah (Eugene, OR: Pickwick Publications, 2022), 77–92.

24 Anno, "On Earth as in Heaven," 83.

mining in that region, this statement of communion expresses a spirituality of struggle and resistance. By claiming the surrounding area as holy, the sticks proclaim a mutuality between earth and humans, present and past.

Of course, the *podong* rite is not Christian liturgy. Yet it corresponds, Anno argues, to the Hebraic tradition of sacred spaces of encounter with God; to the ideas of sabbath and jubilee as rest for people and land; and to the Eucharist. He states, "the feast of life of Christian eschatology is something prefigured in these 'little feasts' of life that the *podong* sticks signal."[25] In a context where Christianization helped to "desacralize" or "disenchant" the Indigenous sacred landscape, Anno sees in the *podong* a sacrament of resistance, an "outward sign of an inward grace" that physically remakes the connection between heaven and earth.[26]

Finally, Catherine Keller, whose notion of "intercarnation" was central to the discussion of Chapter 4, insists that the essential characteristic of this gathered public in liturgy is apophasis: "unsaying," the "negation of any name, dogma, or knowledge of the divine, however true and nonnegotiable it may seem."[27] Apophatic theology approaches God from the perspective of what is unknown and unknowable, rather than what is known. This theology of unknowing is best expressed through contemplative silence. "Consider," she invites, "the world-shifting effects . . . of old contemplative practices, Hindu and Quaker, of silence" as exemplified in the movements of Mohandas Gandhi and Martin Luther King Jr.[28] In moments (or more) of liturgical silence, we might practice the skills of unknowing that allow us to truly hear human and more-than-human others, in what Keller terms "the space of the Holy Spirit."[29] Imagining eco-political community will require a balance of liturgical "unsaying" and "saying."

---

25 Anno, 85.
26 Anno, 79, 91.
27 Keller, *Political Theology of the Earth*, 15.
28 Keller, 122.
29 Keller, 121.

III. COMMUNITIES OF SOLIDARITY

Liturgy, both said and unsaid, has the potential to imagine unimagined possibilities for gathering a new kind of body. As West's incisive critique reminds us, however, this practice is incomplete unless it involves new kinds of communities and new relationships. The eco-political body of Christ must be made concrete in actual communities. New habits of relationship that cross social and ecological boundaries will need to be cultivated and practiced in daily life.

Echoing Copeland's invocation of anamnesis or remembering, ecowomanist ethicist Karen Baker-Fletcher points to the urgent need for a different sort of remembering. "To become whole," she says, "is to re-member," that is, to reincorporate the members of a body.[30] "We have become disembodied from community. We are disembodied from self. We are disembodied from God. We are disembodied from earth." What is needed is re-membering: reestablishing these connections that are the most basic reality of our embodied existence. In this way, we can again become "part of the body of God." For Baker-Fletcher, though, this re-membering happens not primarily in Eucharist or liturgy but in coalition building and community organizing. It happens, that is, in what might be called communities of solidarity.

For many advocates of anti-oppressive communities, solidarity names a praxis, a concrete way of embodying and acting on the deep interconnection among all people and, from an ecological perspective, between humans and the more-than-human world. Recall that this notion of solidarity is central to Copeland's understanding of Eucharist as a habit: Eucharist forms our imaginations and values toward embodied solidarity with the most oppressed and marginalized.[31] For her, solidarity begins with awareness and compassion but necessarily moves toward personal encounter,

---

30 Baker-Fletcher, *Sisters of Dust, Sisters of Spirit*, 57.
31 Copeland, *Enfleshing Freedom*, 125.

intellectual work, and "healing and creative action for change in society."[32] In short, it is nothing less than actively shouldering the oppressions of others.

Christopher Carter builds on Copeland's framework by arguing that for white Christians, the intellectual work of solidarity entails particular demands. It requires overcoming "historical amnesia, the intentional misremembering of the past" that allows white Christians to deny or ignore the historical realities of oppression that have produced their privilege.[33] This involves a critical retelling of history, but more significantly, it involves decentering whiteness from all our narratives. Whiteness, says Carter, "has become an idol that all too many Christians worship, often through the physical or mental image of a white Jesus. . . ." Only by eliminating this idol from our worship and theology can white Christians "see beyond the lens of colonial Christianity" in the way required for real solidarity.[34]

Since whiteness is constructed by excluding not only human but also more-than-human others, solidarity must extend to those more-than-human others. For Carter, this means specifically solidarity with animals: "In order to eliminate rather than just replace the structural evil of racism, we must extend Jesus's call to eliminate the theological and anthropological category of the Other to both human and nonhuman animals."[35] Bioregionalism—a way of organizing geographical space according to ecosystems, watersheds, landscapes, and climate—is one promising tool for building this boundary-crossing solidarity. Bioregionalism, says Carter, invites us to "reinhabit the places [we] already live in by learning to appreciate the unique attributes of [our] own communities. . . . Bioregions are also spaces where nonhuman nature, culture and community intersect. Focusing on such a space gives us a vision of how all life within our communities is deeply connected."[36]

---

32 Copeland, 126.
33 Carter, *The Spirit of Soul Food*, 115–16.
34 Carter, 116.
35 Carter, 113.
36 Carter, 118.

Carter's description of bioregionalism echoes global practices of commoning. Commons are spaces or resources of shared use, to which all members of a community have certain rights. Traditional uses of Appalachian forests, first by Indigenous inhabitants, and then by early settlers, are one example of a historical commons. In the context of a capitalist system that seizes control of such spaces and resources—as coal and timber companies did in the Appalachian example—the commons has become a symbol of resistance, and ultimately a verb. Commoning represents an ethic of relationships that is antithetical to the individualism and consumerism of contemporary capitalism. It is a commitment to mutualism and equitable relationships among humans and between humans and land. But commoning is also concrete communities and practices that enact such cooperative commitments. For example, theologian George Zachariah identifies the resistance of the Standing Rock Sioux Tribe against the Dakota Access Pipeline in 2016 as a practice of commoning.[37] The Sioux's struggle was about a vision of the land as commons, a sacred and living space that encompasses soil, water, air, and creatures. Ultimately, Zachariah insists, commoning is a refusal to accept that there is no alternative to capitalist consumerism.

Efforts toward bioregionalism or commoning as ways of gathering eco-political community can be informed by the specific practices of broad-based community organizing. Broad-based community organizing (BBCO) is a particular tradition of community organizing that—appropriately for our purposes—intentionally gathers community members across categories of religion, class, group affiliation, or interest. BBCO traces its roots to Saul Alinsky, the organizer who founded the Industrial Areas Foundation (IAF) in Chicago in 1940. Alinsky's influence on all forms of democratic activism is hard to overstate, and the development of IAF-style organizing since his time has followed a wide range of trajectories and been assessed in a

---

37 George Zachariah, "Whose Oikos Is It Anyway? Towards a Poromboke Ecotheology of 'Commoning,'" in *Decolonizing Ecotheology: Indigenous and Subaltern Challenges*, ed. S. Lily Mendoza and George Zachariah (Eugene, OR: Pickwick Publications, 2022), 209.

variety of ways by advocates and critics. Central to Alinsky's legacy in BBCO, however, are specific practices with significant implications for relationships, and first among these is the relational meeting.

A relational meeting is a one-to-one conversation that is neither a casual chat nor a narrowly goal-driven interview. Far less is it a recruitment tool or sales pitch. A relational meeting is an intentional individual meeting driven by genuine curiosity about another's values and interests.[38] It is set up with the goal of establishing a "public relationship of solidarity" and ultimately of gathering a collective political body (a public in the sense discussed in earlier chapters), but far from instrumentalizing the other person, this requires real commitment to them as individuals: "The questions are directed with care and concern: often, these stories involve experiences of loss, trauma, and vulnerability. This is the deeply countercultural aspect of the relational meeting. We are not used to being vulnerable in public about the things we collectively hold most dear."[39]

Relational meetings can perform the kind of intellectual work Copeland and Carter insist is necessary for real solidarity. They can invite participants to deep reflection about their narratives and self-conceptions. In particular, they can be an opportunity to reflect critically on social identities and power relations in ways that enable the formation of relationships of solidarity that might transgress and ultimately reconstruct those identities and dynamics.[40]

The one-to-one relational meeting is the basic building block of BBCO; other practices emerge from this foundation.[41] House meetings apply the same sense of solidarity in a more public, outward-facing

---

38 Aaron Stauffer, "The Relational Meeting as a Political and Religious Practice," *Political Theology* 23, no. 1–2 (February 17, 2022): 168.

39 Stauffer, "The Relational Meeting as a Political and Religious Practice," 168.

40 Stauffer, 169.

41 Luke Bretherton, *Resurrecting Democracy: Faith, Citizenship, and the Politics of a Common Life*, illustrated ed. (New York: Cambridge University Press, 2014), 122–47.

context. They represent a moment of awakening, when participants recognize the broader reach and implications of their own experiences. In the terms used in Chapter 3, the house meeting might be seen as the emergence of a public or counterpublic. As these house meetings engage research into the political and technical aspects of issues, they begin to form what Luke Bretherton calls "interpretive communities." In contrast to how knowledge is normally produced and interpreted—by select experts, within a predetermined range of politically palatable options, vetted by polls and focus groups—house meetings and research actions trust the experiences and capabilities of ordinary people, and give them agency over the production and interpretation of knowledge concerning their own communities and bodies.[42] In environmental justice movements, which have significant areas of overlap with BBCO, this production of knowledge often involves "citizen science" or "popular epidemiology": community members gathering and documenting their own data about the environmental harms affecting them.[43] These aspects of BBCO directly respond to the concerns we have seen earlier regarding whiteness as an epistemological project—that is, the way whiteness is perpetuated by maintaining control over what counts as knowledge. BBCO challenges that control by reclaiming from the experts the right to produce and interpret knowledge, be it ecological, political, or theological.

One of the most distinctive and most potentially useful tools that BBCO offers is also one of its most controversial: anger. Beginning with Alinsky, BBCO has consistently affirmed the positive power of anger as a public emotion.[44] Anger, lament, and grief become forces for political mobilization. A characteristic tactic in BBCO meetings is to begin by asking people what makes them angry. This use of anger is so effective precisely because it is so countercultural: "anger goes against core commitments prevalent in the contemporary context: notably, political liberalism's rational consensus orientation,

---

42 Bretherton, *Resurrecting Democracy*, 130.
43 Jenkins, *The Future of Ethics*, 219.
44 Bretherton, *Resurrecting Democracy*, 123–24.

the emphasis among professionals on being an impartial expert, bourgeois notions of respectability, and dominant church cultures of being polite and deferential to those in authority."[45] Anger is a key element in forming ecological counterpublics because it subverts dominant ideas about polite discourse that ultimately serve the status quo; as I described in Chapter 2, objectivity and rationality are the ideological tools of the privileged. This tension is especially difficult for many churches and religious communities—again, particularly predominantly white and other privileged communities—that tend to be so invested in ideas of consensus and polite dialogue. As Alinsky insisted, however, "if you agree with the status quo you represent consensus and . . . if you disagree with them you represent conflict."[46] To the contrary, for Alinsky, real dialogue requires taking sides and, often, expressing anger that demands recognition and respect.

IV. ECOLOGICAL REPARATIONS[47]

The political systems of whiteness—slavery, settler colonialism, and racism—have left their scars on the land. The plantation economy of chattel slavery viewed both Black bodies and the land as resources to be exploited and expended for profit. The monocrop (first tobacco, then cotton) agriculture on which the Southern plantation economy subsisted took what it could from both bodies and land and left them broken. As farms were depleted and eroded, planters simply moved westward, stealing more "fresh" land from Native Americans and leaving feeble soils in their wake. One historian estimates that some parts of the South lost as much as three-quarters of their topsoil. Many of these places remain unable to support productive agriculture

---

45 Bretherton, 124.
46 Bretherton, 125.
47 This section incorporates material from an unpublished white paper on environmental reparations prepared for the Episcopal Church Task Force for the Care of Creation and Environmental Racism in 2020.

today.[48] When these depleted farmlands conspired with political, economic, and physical violence to make subsistence agriculture impossible for the newly freed slaves, they and their descendants either remained in depleted rural communities or migrated to cities, where, as we have seen, they were, and still are, disproportionately exposed to the worst environmental impacts of concentrated populations.

This history of slavery's environmental legacy is just one example of the lasting environmental impacts of white supremacy and settler colonialism. Others have been documented throughout this book. When Indigenous people were forcibly removed from the land, the small-scale, regenerative agriculture that many tribes practiced was lost, as Native Americans were moved again and again to more concentrated and less arable land. Again, the land suffered.

Climate change, too, can be seen as the enduring atmospheric accumulations of centuries of colonialism. Climate inequalities are built on long-established patterns of injustice created by military conquest, economic exploitation, and the slave trade. The military might needed to maintain the political economies of colonialism has been a major contributor to climate change, and the current global fossil fuel economy is built on those centuries-old patterns. In many ways global climate change represents the lasting ecological scars of colonialism and neocolonialism.[49]

In these examples, people and land are devastated in ways that endure. More troublingly, though, relationships with the land are severed. People are uprooted from the places they know; deep-seated ecological knowledge is lost and replaced with social and ecological violence. People and land still bear these scars. The historical injustices of racism and settler colonialism are not tallied on some hypothetical balance sheet; they are indelibly written on the land and in the atmosphere.

---

48 Roger G. Kennedy, *Mr. Jefferson's Lost Cause: Land, Farmers, Slavery, and the Louisiana Purchase* (New York: Oxford University Press, 2003), 233.
49 Amitav Ghosh, *The Nutmeg's Curse: Parables for a Planet in Crisis* (Chicago: University of Chicago Press, 2021), 126.

Reparations are a mechanism for holding the systems of whiteness and their beneficiaries accountable for these historical injustices and their enduring effects. If reparations are about seeking justice for historical and present wrongs, then they need to be conceived of as having an ecological character, because those wrongs have an ecological character. Whiteness has harmed—and continues to harm—people of color and the environment, and it harms them jointly, together, partly by violating the relations that connect them. Reparations need to address this joint harm and restore what has been violated.

Traditionally, reparations have been understood in two ways, which philosopher Olúfẹ́mi O. Táíwò describes as the "harm repair" and "relationship repair" arguments.[50] Harm repair arguments view reparations as principally about restitution: present-day victims are harmed by past wrongs, and therefore deserve to be "made whole," restored to some more equitable position they would occupy if not for the past wrong. Relationship repair arguments, on the other hand, view reparations as principally about restoring a relationship that has been breached: historical wrongs have damaged the moral relations between the victims and the victimizers and their respective descendants, and those relations can only be restored through concrete steps toward repair. Relationship repair arguments, in turn, fall into two categories. Debt repayment views argue that a moral debt exists that must be repaid for the two parties to restore relations. Communicative repair views say that the important effect of concrete reparations is to indicate genuine commitment to restoring the relationship, and that refusal to offer reparations signals a refusal to recognize the seriousness of the injury.

Each of these categories presents certain strengths and shortcomings. For example, relationship repair views avoid the complicated calculus of trying to establish a hypothetical baseline—that is, of trying to figure out how much slavery has harmed contemporary descendants of slaves, and therefore how much restitution is owed.

---

50 Táíwò, *Reconsidering Reparations*, 124.

At the same time, they may be seen as subtly shifting the focus away from material compensation to more symbolic forms of redress.[51]

A notion of debt repayment or restitution for historical wrongs is crucial for one area of ecological reparations. A serious effort to decolonize Christian environmentalism requires returning land taken by coercion and force to its original inhabitants. Most churches in the United States occupy such stolen land. Talk of environmental justice and anti-oppressive environmentalism rings hollow if it is not accompanied by concrete actions to return land to Indigenous people. As Mark Charles argues persuasively, denunciations of the doctrine of discovery, like those issued by many mainline denominations, are disingenuous unless those same churches are willing to make a commitment not to rely on the doctrine in court if sued for their lands by Native tribes.[52] If such a radical step seems impossible, this only demonstrates just how deeply formed our imaginations are by settler colonialism and whiteness.

Nonetheless, land restitution is complicated. If it is not to be merely a symbolic gesture or to reinscribe colonial dynamics, it must meaningfully return control and agency over the land to Native Americans. This requires, first, learning about the original inhabitants of a place and working to establish relationships with them. It requires taking the time to understand their desires and visions. There are various models for the actual transfer of control of land to its Indigenous owners, from straightforward land transfer to the establishment of land trusts and other cooperative arrangements. What is essential is that at every step of the process, agency and informed consent reside with the Native communities.

Land restitution is a good example of the moral force of a harm repair or restitution model of reparations. More comprehensive efforts for ecological reparations, though, call for a broader vision of what reparations can do. Táíwò proposes what he calls a constructive view that calls for nothing less than "worldmaking." Describing

---

51 Táíwò, 136.
52 Charles and Rah, *Unsettling Truths*, 185.

the objective that reparations must fulfill, he says, "if slavery and colonialism built the world and its current basic scheme of social injustice, the proper task of social justice is no smaller: it is, quite literally, to remake the world."[53] Such a view of reparations is informed by history; it demands that the costs of building that new, just world fall on those who inherit the "moral liabilities" of the institutions and people responsible for slavery and colonialism.[54] But its focus is forward-looking. Its goal is a "global community thoroughly structured by non-domination," a world where everyone is guaranteed a basic level of flourishing and self-determination.[55]

The key issue for Táíwò's account of reparations is climate change. Climate change perpetuates the historical inequalities of colonialism, and exacerbates the unequal distribution of all sorts of benefits and burdens. Formerly colonized countries are more vulnerable to climate change and pollution than those that were never colonized.[56] Within countries, too, communities of color already suffer more from the harms of climate change, and the United States' first climate refugees have been Native American communities forced from their land by sea-level rise.[57] At the same time, existing patterns of inequality rooted in colonialism—such as in wealth, political power, and social stability—will all be magnified by the effects of climate change. As droughts, famines, and floods make many areas uninhabitable, climate migration will lead to increased political instability and conflict. The worldmaking project of reparations requires addressing climate injustice.

A first step toward ecological reparations is straightforward: cash transfers. This is what most people imagine when they think of reparations, and it can be an effective way to guarantee the basic universal level of flourishing Táíwò calls for while specifically targeting those whose flourishing has been undermined by the

---

53 Táíwò, *Reconsidering Reparations*, 67.
54 Táíwò, 98.
55 Táíwò, 102.
56 Táíwò, 64–71.
57 Táíwò, 161–62.

legacies of slavery and colonialism.[58] Other strategies take aim at rectifying the unjust distribution of economic and political power. The wealthy nations most responsible for climate change have repeatedly made commitments to fund the climate resilience of poorer nations. Yet they have consistently failed to make good on those commitments, while at the same time, they have used climate adaptation projects to saddle poorer nations with sovereign debt. Ecological reparations demand that the wealthy nations release poorer climate-vulnerable nations from these unjust debt obligations while also fulfilling their own commitment to make good on their climate debt. While these steps are obviously beyond the reach of individual communities, churches and denominations should be vocal in advocating for them.

Divestment from fossil fuels and reinvestment in projects of justice and sustainability, on the other hand, are well within the capacity of individual churches and denominations. Divestment from fossil fuel companies is a matter of extricating our financial resources from an industry built on generating insecurity. This is a moral necessity. More significantly, though, it is about reinvesting those resources in a more just world.[59] While one obvious option for reinvestment is renewable energy alternatives, those alternatives are not always unproblematic, and communities and individuals should be diligent about which investments to make. But because ecological reparations are about a broader vision of flourishing, and because the effects of environmental injustice and climate colonialism are so pervasive, options for reinvesting in a just and sustainable world can be broader than just energy companies. Churches and individuals might invest in community organizations and environmental projects in communities of color that aim to keep decision-making agency and control within the communities. According to Táíwò, "green investments in Black and Indigenous communities *are* climate-responsible investments."[60]

---

58 Táíwò, 175.
59 Táíwò, 182.
60 Táíwò, 182 (italics in original).

Divestment and reinvestment, climate funding, and even cash transfers are not unique to reparations efforts. Framing them as reparations, however, gives them a different moral significance. What the concept of ecological reparations entails is, first, a recognition that racial reconciliation requires environmental reconciliation; second, the acknowledgment that environmental work that does not address historic racism and settler colonialism perpetuates white supremacy; and, third, the understanding that this work is not optional but rather is demanded by basic justice as a rectification of historic and enduring wrongs. As Táíwò's relationship repair model affirms, restoring the human and ecological relationships sundered by racism and colonialism requires concrete actions to address the lasting harms these systems of whiteness have caused. This is why ecological reparations, together with practices of solidarity and transformative liturgy, are necessary tools for gathering communities as the eco-political body of Christ.

V. CHALLENGING WHITENESS, BECOMING NATURALIZED

Ultimately, what can white Christians and predominantly white Christian institutions do to dismantle the whiteness of our environmentalism and ecotheology? Can the inheritors of the construction of whiteness, the beneficiaries of systems of racism and colonialism, step outside of that construction to become indigenous to our places?

This is a question that Robin Wall Kimmerer ponders in *Braiding Sweetgrass*. It is simply too painful, she says, to ignore the past and invite settler society to consider themselves indigenous, no matter how good the intention or how sincere the effort. "No amount of time or caring changes history or substitutes for soul-deep fusion with the land."[61] White Christians and predominantly white churches need to bear this in mind. Restoring community, gathering an

---

61 Kimmerer, *Braiding Sweetgrass*, 213.

eco-political body, solidarity and reparations—none of these can undo the past. The social and ecological scars of slavery, racism, and settler colonialism can never be completely erased.

We who are not native to North America can, however, become what Willie Jennings calls "second readers." Recall that for Jennings, Christians come to the creation accounts of the Hebrew Scriptures as second readers, inheriting these texts and learning about the Creator from those to whom the stories were originally entrusted. Supersessionism is when Christians forget this relationship and imagine themselves to be first readers. In the same way, white Christians can learn to be second readers of our places, entering the physical and spiritual world of others and learning from them in what he describes as "a pedagogy of joining."[62]

In her reflection on the subject, Kimmerer invites us to contemplate the common plantain, *Plantago major*. Called "White Man's Footstep" in Potawatomi, the plantain is a nonnative plant that arrived with the first settlers. As the Native tribes learned from the plant, they discovered that it could be eaten and had a variety of medicinal uses. "This wise and generous plant," Kimmerer reflects, "became an honored member of the plant community. It's a foreigner, an immigrant, but after five hundred years of living as a good neighbor, people forget that kind of thing."[63] Unlike other nonnative species like kudzu and garlic mustard, plantain coexists with native species and finds its niche in its new place.

Plants like plantain are said to be "naturalized." Perhaps settlers can become naturalized to their place as well.

Being naturalized to place means to live as if this is the land that feeds you, as if these are the streams from which you drink, that build your body and fill your spirit. To become naturalized is to know that your ancestors lie in this ground. Here you will give your gifts and meet your responsibilities. To become naturalized is to live as if your children's

---

62 Jennings, "Reframing the World: Toward an Actual Christian Doctrine of Creation," 394.

63 Kimmerer, *Braiding Sweetgrass*, 214.

future matters, to take care of the land as if our lives and the lives of all our relatives depend on it. Because they do.[64]

My hope is that by gathering an eco-political community in the way that I have described, through practices of joining like those above, white Christians may begin to become naturalized. The ruptures caused by whiteness, by settler colonialism and racism, are deep. They infect our institutions and polities, our worship, our theologies, our very imaginations and ways of knowing. This is why simple awareness or symbolic declarations like the repudiations of the doctrine of discovery do not begin to challenge the whiteness of Christian environmentalism. This is why it takes deep practice, habituation, formation in liturgy, active solidarity, and concrete reparations. It takes forming new imaginations that are capable of envisioning societies and relationships free of hierarchies and domination.

But plantain will never be native to these soils. Second readers are not first readers. As Christopher Carter confirms, for white people solidarity requires us to decenter our own interests, our own stories and experience.[65] The construction of whiteness is the centering of a certain experience or perspective as normative, accomplished so completely that that perspective seems universal to those who are identified with it—it seems natural. To be in solidarity with people of color, to be second readers, therefore requires ongoing intentional effort to decenter white experiences and center the stories of others. To become naturalized to place requires, in a sense, denaturalizing whiteness, recognizing it as a construction, realizing that there are other ways of knowing and imagining. And it requires constant attention, listening to and learning from these other ways. It requires learning to join, learning to follow, as the plantain follows—"White Man's Footstep," now naturalized in its new soil.

---

64 Kimmerer, 214–15.
65 Carter, *The Spirit of Soul Food*, 116.

Conclusion: Trees of Gathering

We end, just as we began, with the tree of life. In the final chapter of Revelation, the tree of life presents a striking image of healing and harmony. John of Patmos tells us the tree grows on either side of a river of crystal-clear water, and that it yields twelve kinds of fruit, one every month. "And the leaves of the tree," writes John, "are for the healing of the nations. Nothing accursed will be found there any more" (Rev 22:2–3). He goes on to describe the glory of this new creation: "There will be no more night; they need no light of lamp or sun, for the Lord God will be their light, and they will reign forever and ever" (Rev 22:5).

Trees gather. They gather nutrients, soil and water, sunlight and air into their cells, and in the process, they connect to thousands of other species. Visually, their branching crowns and spreading roots image reaching, extending, and including. Biologically, their roots and leaves are networked with fungi and bacteria, connecting them with the whole biological community. Biologist and writer David George Haskell describes trees' gathering as an example of "unselfing": a self-transcendence that can free us from the boundaries of identity for a life of community, in what he calls an ethic of belonging.[1]

How appropriate, then, that the symbol of the new creation, a reality of unity and reconciliation, is a tree. The tree of life in Revelation is a tree that gathers people to God. The word "nations" here

---

1 David George Haskell, *The Songs of Trees: Stories from Nature's Great Connectors* (New York: Viking, 2017), 149–53.

refers to the Gentiles, those outside Israel's relationship with God. In the new creation, they are joined to Israel and to God; the leaves of the tree are the symbol of this joining.

For Willie James Jennings, the question of how the Gentiles are joined to Israel is the crucial question in the face of the colonialist construction of race.[2] The joining described throughout the Bible, expressed paradigmatically in Jesus and culminating with the joining of Revelation, must overcome the separations produced by the construction of whiteness. It must overcome the abstracting of people into categories that can be hierarchically ordered, and the reduction of places to a totalizing ideal of interchangeable space. It must be a joining of bodies in particular places, in light of God's whole history with God's people of Israel. This joining, understood in ecological terms, is the eco-political community I have been describing throughout this book. This is what is symbolized by the tree of life of the book of Revelation.

There is another tree whose gathering challenges whiteness. A "witness tree" is a tree that was present at a significant moment in history and survives. Often bearing scars or markers of their past, these trees are protected by communities for the history they preserve. Many of the trees recall past battles, but the term can also be applied to trees that are preserved to bear witness to the evils of slavery and lynching.[3] Virginia Richards, a photographer who has documented the canals constructed with slave labor in South Carolina, describes what witness trees, and the larger landscape, can do for memory. "My hope," she says "is that images can convey a landscape scarred with secrets: river baptisms, planting seasons, torture, dancing, prayers, African dialects, poverty, massacres,

---

2 Jennings, *The Christian Imagination*, 250–88.

3 Imani Perry, "What the Haunting 'Inner Passage' Represented to the Enslaved," *Smithsonian Magazine*, March 2022, accessed May 14, 2022, https://www.smithsonianmag.com/travel/what-haunting-inner-passage-represented-to-enslaved-180979552/; Jared Farmer, "Witness to a Hanging: California's Haunted Trees," *Boom* 3, no. 1 (May 1, 2013): 70–79, https://doi.org/10.1525/boom.2013.3.1.70.

lynchings. The land remembers but cannot speak."[4] As an article about Richards's images reflects, "These oaks are the only creatures still alive today that witnessed these sights, and by looking at them, we witness their testimony. They tell us of the people who sheltered in their branches, or behind their thick brown trunks, breathing heavily, wet with sweat, dew on the grass and moisture in the air."[5]

The witness trees gathered this air, the dew, the sweat, the breath, into their cells. Where they stand today, they join these fragments of history with the current landscape and its inhabitants. They literally and physically join the past with the present. They perform the same gathering as the tree of Revelation—a gathering that does not deny the suffering of the past but rather draws it in: "Just as Jesus drew into himself the energy of a violent world in order to heal that energy and turn it toward the good, so the communion envisioned by his body draws into itself the agon [struggle or conflict, but also gathering[6]] of peoples in order to turn strife into desire."[7]

The word "radical" refers to roots—to getting to the root, the foundation of an issue. These two trees express a radical imagination in multiple senses. It is an imagination that is rooted: it has roots, roots that join it to the whole community of life, that manifest the gathering proper to trees. And it is foundational: it goes to the very roots of our ways of understanding life and relationship. This imagination crosses the boundaries between literal, physical connection and spiritual connection. The trees' gathering physically embodies the transcendent relationships that join human and more-than-human lives across space and across time.

These images of gathering are precisely the kind of radical imagination required to envision and enact the eco-political body of Christ. Whiteness operates by establishing divisions and hierarchies; the trees represent the connectedness that is the true nature of reality,

---

4 Perry, "What the Haunting 'Inner Passage' Represented to the Enslaved," 46.

5 Perry, 51.

6 "Agon," Merriam-Webster, https://www.merriam-webster.com/dictionary/agon.

7 Jennings, *The Christian Imagination*, 274.

and the vision to which God calls us. Karen-Baker Fletcher gives poignant voice to this radical vocation: "We are called into a vision of New Creation, a moment by moment, day by day, generation by generation process of earthly and spiritual renewal. . . . By the Spirit, we are called to realize the apocalyptic vision of a new heaven and a new earth by being wise stewards of body, dust, and spirit, engaged in the task of healing."[8]

---

8 Karen Baker-Fletcher, *Sisters of Dust, Sisters of Spirit*, 127.

Bibliography

"Acts of Convention: Resolution # 2009-D035." Accessed September 22, 2021. https://www.episcopalarchives.org/cgi-bin/acts/acts_resolution.pl?resolution=2009-D035.

Anno, Ferdinand. "On Earth as in Heaven: The Earth in the Podong Leitourgia of the Post-Human Commune." In *Decolonizing Ecotheology: Indigenous and Subaltern Challenges*, edited by S. Lily Mendoza and George Zachariah, 77–92. Eugene, OR: Pickwick Publications, 2022.

Anzaldúa, Gloria. *Light in the Dark/Luz en lo Oscuro: Rewriting Identity, Spirituality, Reality*, illustrated ed. Edited by AnaLouise Keating. Durham, NC: Duke University Press, 2015.

——. *Borderlands/La Frontera: The New Mestiza*, 4th ed. San Francisco: Aunt Lute Books, 2012.

Associated Press. "Sierra Club Apologizes for Founder John Muir's Racist Views." Accessed May 9, 2022. https://www.nbcnews.com/news/nbcblk/sierra-club-apologizes-founder-john-muir-s-racist-views-n1234695.

Azaransky, Sarah. "Impossible, Inadequate, and Indispensable: What North American Christian Social Ethics Can Learn from Postcolonial Theory." *Journal of the Society of Christian Ethics* 37, no. 1 (January 1, 2017): 46.

Baker-Fletcher, Karen. *Sisters of Dust, Sisters of Spirit: Womanist Wordings on God and Creation*. Minneapolis: Fortress Press, 1998.

Batteau, Allen. *The Invention of Appalachia*. The Anthropology of Form and Meaning. Tucson: University of Arizona Press, 1990.

Bauckham, Richard. "The Incarnation and the Cosmic Christ." In *Incarnation: On the Scope and Depth of Christology*, edited by Niels Henrik Gregersen, 25–58. Minneapolis: Fortress Press, 2015.

Baugh, Amanda J. *God and the Green Divide: Religious Environmentalism in Black and White*. Oakland: University of California Press, 2017.

Bauman, Whitney A. "Creatio Ex Nihilo, Terra Nullius, and the Erasure of Presence." In *Ecospirit: Religions and Philosophies for the Earth*, edited by Laurel Kearns and Catherine Keller, 353–72. Transdisciplinary Theological Colloquia. New York: Fordham University Press, 2007.

Bauman, Whitney A., and Kevin J. O'Brien. *Environmental Ethics and Uncertainty: Wrestling with Wicked Problems*. Abingdon, UK: Routledge, 2019.

Behr, John. "Saint Athanasius on 'Incarnation.'" In *Incarnation: On the Scope and Depth of Christology*, edited by Niels Henrik Gregersen, 79–98. Minneapolis: Fortress Press, 2015.

Berry, Wendell. *The Unsettling of America: Culture & Agriculture*, reprint ed. Berkeley: Counterpoint, 2015.

Bohannon, Richard R., II, and Kevin J. O'Brien. "Saving the World (and the People in It, Too): Religion in Eco-Justice and Environmental Justice." In *Inherited Land: The Changing Grounds of Religion and Ecology*, edited by Whitney A. Bauman, Richard R. Bohannon II, and Kevin J. O'Brien, 171–87. Eugene, OR: Pickwick Publications, 2011.

Bretherton, Luke. *Resurrecting Democracy: Faith, Citizenship, and the Politics of a Common Life*, illustrated ed. New York: Cambridge University Press, 2014.

Brinton, Henry G. "Revelation 21:1–22:7." *Interpretation: A Journal of Bible & Theology* 70, no. 1 (January 2016): 84–86.

Cady, Linell E. *Religion, Theology, and American Public Life*. Albany: SUNY Press, 1993.

Carter, Christopher. "Blood in the Soil: The Racial, Racist, and Religious Dimensions of Environmentalism." In *The Bloomsbury Handbook of Religion and Nature: The Elements*, edited by Laura Hobgood and Whitney Bauman, 45–62. Bloomsbury Handbooks in Religion. London: Bloomsbury Academic, 2018.

———. *The Spirit of Soul Food: Race, Faith, and Food Justice*. Urbana: University of Illinois Press, 2021.

Charles, Mark, and Soong-Chan Rah. *Unsettling Truths: The Ongoing, Dehumanizing Legacy of the Doctrine of Discovery*, illustrated ed. Downers Grove, IL: IVP Books, 2019.

Chavez, David. "Lessons from the Border." The School of Theology, The University of the South, Sewanee, TN, October 26, 2021.

Clay, Elonda. "How Does It Feel to Be an Environmental Problem? Studying Religion and Ecology in the African Diaspora." In *Inherited Land: The Changing Grounds of Religion and Ecology*, edited by Whitney A. Bauman, Richard R. Bohannon II, and Kevin J. O'Brien, 148–70. Eugene, OR: Pickwick Publications, 2011.

Cole, Luke W., and Sheila R. Foster. *From the Ground Up: Environmental Racism and the Rise of the Environmental Justice Movement*. Critical America. New York: NYU Press, 2001.

Collins, John J. *The Apocalyptic Imagination: An Introduction to Jewish Apocalyptic Literature*, 3rd ed. Grand Rapids, MI: Eerdmans, 2016.

———. *Introduction to the Hebrew Bible: The Writings*, 3rd ed. Minneapolis: Fortress Press, 2019.

Cone, James H. "Whose Earth Is It Anyway?" *CrossCurrents* 50, no. 1/2 (April 1, 2000): 36–46.

Copeland, M. Shawn. *Enfleshing Freedom: Body, Race, and Being*. Minneapolis: Fortress Press, 2009.

Crutzen, Paul J., and Eugene F. Stoermer. "The Anthropocene." *Global Change Newsletter* 41, no. 1 (2000).

Davis, Ellen F. *Scripture, Culture, and Agriculture: An Agrarian Reading of the Bible*. New York: Cambridge University Press, 2009.

Deane-Drummond, Celia. *A Primer in Ecotheology: Theology for a Fragile Earth.* Cascade Companions 37. Eugene, OR: Cascade Books, 2017.

Deloria, Vine, Jr. *Spirit and Reason: The Vine Deloria Jr. Reader.* Edited by Sam Scinta and Kristen Foehner. Golden, CO: Fulcrum Publishing, 1999.

Demuth, Bathsheba. "Reindeer at the End of the World." *Emergence* magazine, July 5, 2020. Accessed November 15, 2021. https://emergencemagazine.org/essay/reindeer-at-the-end-of-the-world/.

Dewey, John. *The Public and Its Problems.* New York: Henry Holt & Company, 1927.

Douglas, Kelly Brown. *The Black Christ: 25th Anniversary Edition.* Maryknoll, NY: Orbis, 2021.

———. *Stand Your Ground: Black Bodies and the Justice of God.* Maryknoll, NY: Orbis, 2015.

"El Pueblo Para El Aire y Agua Limpio v. County of Kings." *The Environmental Law Reporter,* December 30, 1991. Accessed August 20, 2020. https://elr.info/sites/default/files/litigation/22.20357.htm.

Farmer, Jared. "Witness to a Hanging: California's Haunted Trees." *Boom* 3, no. 1 (May 1, 2013): 70–79. https://doi.org/10.1525/boom.2013.3.1.70.

Feagin, Joe R. *The White Racial Frame: Centuries of Racial Framing and Counter-Framing.* New York: Routledge, 2009.

Fraser, Nancy. "Rethinking the Public Sphere: A Contribution to the Critique of Actually Existing Democracy." In *Habermas and the Public Sphere,* edited by Craig Calhoun, 109–42. Cambridge, MA: The MIT Press, 1992.

Fredericks, Sarah, and Kevin J. O'Brien. "The Importance and Limits of Taking Science Seriously: Data and Uncertainty in Religion and Ecology." In *Inherited Land: The Changing Grounds of Religion and Ecology,* edited by Whitney A. Bauman, Richard R. Bohannon II, and Kevin J. O'Brien. Eugene, OR: Pickwick Publications, 2011.

Freeman, Jon. "Che Apalache's Leader Joe Troop Pleads for Empathy in New Song 'Mercy for Migrants.'" *Rolling Stone*, August 11, 2021. Accessed October 28, 2021. https://www.rollingstone.com/music/music-country/joe-troop-che-apalache-mercy-for-migrants-1210570/.

Gebara, Ivone. *Longing for Running Water: Ecofeminism and Liberation.* Translated by David Molineaux. Minneapolis: Fortress Press, 1999.

Ghosh, Amitav. *The Nutmeg's Curse: Parables for a Planet in Crisis.* Chicago: University of Chicago Press, 2021.

Gilio-Whitaker, Dina. *As Long as Grass Grows: The Indigenous Fight for Environmental Justice, from Colonization to Standing Rock,* reprint ed. Boston: Beacon Press, 2020.

Gregersen, Niels Henrik. "The Cross of Christ in an Evolutionary World." *Dialog: A Journal of Theology* 40, no. 3 (September 2001): 192.

———. "The Extended Body of Christ:" In *Incarnation: On the Scope and Depth of Christology,* edited by Niels Henrik Gregersen, 225–52. Minneapolis: Fortress Press, 2015. https://doi.org/10.2307/j.ctt13wwwk5.14.

———. "Introduction." In *Incarnation: On the Scope and Depth of Christology,* edited by Niels Henrik Gregersen, 1–22. Minneapolis: Fortress Press, 2015. https://doi.org/10.2307/j.ctt13wwwk5.4.

Grizzle, Raymond E., and Christopher B. Barrett. "The One Body of Christian Environmentalism." *Zygon* 33, no. 2 (June 1, 1998): 233.

Gutting, Gary. *Foucault: A Very Short Introduction.* Oxford: Oxford University Press, 2005.

Haskell, David George. *The Songs of Trees: Stories from Nature's Great Connectors.* New York: Viking, 2017.

Hulac, Benjamin. "Tobacco and Oil Industries Used Same Researchers to Sway Public." *Scientific American*, July 20, 2016. Accessed May 25, 2022. https://www.scientificamerican.com/article/tobacco-and-oil-industries-used-same-researchers-to-sway-public1/.

Indigenous Values Initiative. "Repudiations by Faith Communities." Doctrine of Discovery, July 30, 2018. https://doctrineofdiscovery. org/faith-communities/.

Jacobs, Alan. "The Watchmen." *Harper's Magazine*, September 2016. https://harpers.org/archive/2016/09/the-watchmen/.

Jantzen, Matt R. *God, Race, and History: Liberating Providence.* Lanham: Lexington Books, 2021.

Jenkins, Willis. *Ecologies of Grace: Environmental Ethics and Christian Theology.* Oxford: Oxford University Press, 2008.

———. *The Future of Ethics: Sustainability, Social Justice, and Religious Creativity.* Washington, DC: Georgetown University Press, 2013.

Jennings, Willie James. *After Whiteness: An Education in Belonging,* illustrated ed. Grand Rapids, MI: Eerdmans, 2020.

———. *The Christian Imagination: Theology and the Origins of Race.* New Haven, CT: Yale University Press, 2011.

———. "Reframing the World: Toward an Actual Christian Doctrine of Creation." *International Journal of Systematic Theology* 21, no. 4 (October 1, 2019): 388–407. https://doi.org/10.1111/ ijst.12385.

Joerstad, Mari. *The Hebrew Bible and Environmental Ethics: Humans, Nonhumans, and the Living Landscape.* Cambridge and New York: Cambridge University Press, 2019.

Johnson, Elizabeth A. "Jesus and the Cosmos." In *Incarnation: On the Scope and Depth of Christology,* edited by Niels Henrik Gregersen, 133–56. Minneapolis: Fortress Press, 2015.

Kaplan, M. Lindsay. *Figuring Racism in Medieval Christianity.* Oxford: Oxford University Press, 2019.

Kearns, Laurel. "Ecology and Religious Environmentalism in the United States." In *The Oxford Encyclopedia of Religion in America,* edited by John Corrigan, vol. 2, 604–46. New York: Oxford University Press, 2018.

———. "Religious Climate Activism in the United States." In *Religion in Environmental and Climate Change: Suffering, Values, Lifestyles,* edited by Dieter Gerten and Sigurd Bergmann, 132– 51. London: Bloomsbury Academic, 2012.

———. "Saving the Creation: Christian Environmentalism in the United States." *Sociology of Religion* 57, no. 1 (March 1, 1996): 55–70. https://doi.org/10.2307/3712004.

Keller, Catherine. *Political Theology of the Earth: Our Planetary Emergency and the Struggle for a New Public.* New York: Columbia University Press, 2018.

Kennedy, Roger G. *Mr. Jefferson's Lost Cause: Land, Farmers, Slavery, and the Louisiana Purchase.* New York: Oxford University Press, 2003.

Kimmerer, Robin Wall. *Braiding Sweetgrass: Indigenous Wisdom, Scientific Knowledge and the Teachings of Plants.* Minneapolis: Milkweed Editions, 2015.

The Long March to Rome. "The Creator Has Been Heard." Accessed September 22, 2021. http://longmarchtorome.com/the-creator-has-been-heard/.

McFague, Sallie. *The Body of God: An Ecological Theology.* Minneapolis: Fortress Press, 1993.

McGivern, Mary Ann. "Indian Nations Ask Pope Francis to Rescind Doctrine of Discovery." *National Catholic Reporter,* December 28, 2018. Accessed November 4, 2022. https://www.ncronline.org/news/opinion/ncr-today/indian-nations-ask-pope-francis-rescind-doctrine-discovery.

Mendoza, S. Lily, and George Zachariah. "Introduction." In *Decolonizing Ecotheology: Indigenous and Subaltern Challenges,* edited by S. Lily Mendoza and George Zachariah, 1–16. Eugene, OR: Pickwick Publications, 2022.

Middleton, J. Richard. *A New Heaven and a New Earth: Reclaiming Biblical Eschatology,* illustrated ed. Grand Rapids, MI: Baker Academic, 2014.

Mignolo, Walter D., and Catherine E. Walsh. *On Decoloniality: Concepts, Analytics, Praxis.* Durham, NC: Duke University Press, 2018.

Millard, Egan. "Musician Joe Troop Releases Song, Video Inspired by Episcopal-Supported Migrant Shelter." *Episcopal News Service* (blog), September 20, 2021. Accessed November 4, 2022. https://www.episcopalnewsservice.org/2021/09/20/musician-joe-troop-releases-song-video-inspired-by-episcopal-supported-migrant-shelter/.

Milman, Oliver. "Buffalo Suspect May Be Latest Mass Shooter Motivated by 'Eco-Fascism.'" *The Guardian*, May 17, 2022. Accessed November 4, 2022. https://www.theguardian.com/us-news/2022/may/17/buffalo-shooting-suspect-eco-fascism.

Moore, Stephen D. "The Revelation to John." In *A Postcolonial Commentary on the New Testament Writings*, edited by Fernando F. Segovia and R. S. Sugirtharajah, 436–54. London: T and T Clark, 2007.

Nash, Roderick Frazier. *Wilderness and the American Mind*, 5th ed. New Haven, CT: Yale University Press, 2014.

Norton, Bryan G. *Sustainability: A Philosophy of Adaptive Ecosystem Management*, new ed. Chicago: University of Chicago Press, 2005.

Perry, Imani. "What the Haunting 'Inner Passage' Represented to the Enslaved." *Smithsonian Magazine*, March 2022. Accessed May 14, 2022. https://www.smithsonianmag.com/travel/what-haunting-inner-passage-represented-to-enslaved-180979552/.

Pugliese, Joseph. *Biopolitics of the More-Than-Human*. Forensic Ecologies of Violence. Durham, NC: Duke University Press, 2020. https://doi.org/10.2307/j.ctv17z84k4.4.

Quijano, Aníbal. "Coloniality and Modernity/Rationality." *Cultural Studies* 21, no. 2–3 (March 1, 2007): 169. https://doi.org/10.1080/09502380601164353.

Rasmussen, Larry. "Environmental Racism and Environmental Justice: Moral Theory in the Making?" *Journal of the Society of Christian Ethics* 24, no. 1 (2004): 3–28.

Rivera, Mayra. *The Touch of Transcendence: A Postcolonial Theology of God*. Louisville, KY: Westminster John Knox Press, 2007.

Roland Guzmán, Carla E. "Dismantling the Discourses of the 'Black Legend' as They Still Function in the Episcopal Church: A Case against Latinx Ministries as a Program of the Church." *Anglican Theological Review* 101, no. 4 (October 1, 2019): 603–24.

Rossing, Barbara R., and Johan Buitendag. "Life in Its Fullness: Ecology, Eschatology and Ecodomy in a Time of Climate Change." *HTS Teologiese Studies/Theological Studies* 76, no. 1 (November 1, 2020): e1–9. https://doi.org/10.4102/hts.v76i1.6245.

Rotondaro, Vinnie. "Doctrine of Discovery: A Scandal in Plain Sight." *National Catholic Reporter*, September 5, 2015. Accessed November 4, 2022. https://www.ncronline.org/news/justice/doctrine-discovery-scandal-plain-sight.

Shrader-Frechette, Kristin S. *Environmental Justice: Creating Equality, Reclaiming Democracy*. Oxford: Oxford University Press, 2002.

Shrader-Frechette, Kristin, and Andrew M. Biondo. "Data-Quality Assessment Signals Toxic-Site Safety Threats and Environmental Injustices." *International Journal of Environmental Research and Public Health* 18, no. 4 (February 1, 2021): 2012. https://doi.org/10.3390/ijerph18042012.

———. "Health Misinformation about Toxic-Site Harm: The Case for Independent-Party Testing to Confirm Safety." *International Journal of Environmental Research and Public Health* 18, no. 8 (April 1, 2021): 3882. https://doi.org/10.3390/ijerph18083882.

Snær Magnason, Andri, and Anni Ólafsdóttir. *Apausalypse* (film). Elsku Run Productions, 2020. https://emergencemagazine.org/film/apausalypse/.

———. "Apausalypse: Dispatch from Iceland." *Emergence* magazine, May 21, 2020. Accessed November 10, 2021. https://emergencemagazine.org/essay/apausalypse-dispatch-from-iceland/.

Southgate, Christopher. "Depth, Sign and Destiny." In *Incarnation: On the Scope and Depth of Christology*, edited by Niels Henrik Gregersen, 203–24. Minneapolis: Fortress Press, 2015.

Stauffer, Aaron. "The Relational Meeting as a Political and Religious Practice." *Political Theology* 23, no. 1–2 (February 17, 2022): 167–73. https://doi.org/10.1080/1462317X.2021.1899704.

Taber-Hamilton, Rachel K. "When Creation Is Sacred: Restoring the Indigenous Jesus." *Anglican Theological Review* 103, no. 2 (2021): 166–85.

Táíwò, Olúfẹ́mi O. *Reconsidering Reparations*. New York: Oxford University Press, 2022.

Taylor, Bron. *Dark Green Religion: Nature Spirituality and the Planetary Future*. Berkeley: University of California Press, 2010.

———. "Wilderness, Spirituality and Biodiversity in North America— Tracing an Environmental History from Occidental Roots to Earth Day." In *Wilderness in Mythology and Religion: Approaching Religious Spatialities, Cosmologies, and Ideas of Wild Nature*, edited by Laura Feldt, 293–324. Boston: De Gruyter, 2012.

Taylor, Dorceta E. "Women of Color, Environmental Justice, and Ecofeminism." In *Ecofeminism: Women, Culture, Nature*, edited by Karen Warren, 38–81. Bloomington: Indiana University Press, 1997.

Thompson, Andrew R. H. "Environmental Justice as Counter-public Theology: Reflections for a Postpandemic Public." *American Journal of Theology & Philosophy* 41, no. 2–3 (May 1, 2020): 114–32. https://doi.org/10.5406/amerjtheophil.41.2-3.0114.

Tuck, Eve, and K. Wayne Yang, "Decolonization Is Not a Metaphor." *Decolonization: Indigeneity, Education, and Society* 1, no. 1 (September 8, 2012): 1–40.

United Church of Christ Commission for Racial Justice. *Toxic Wastes and Race in the United States*. United Church of Christ, 1987.

United Church of Christ Justice and Witness Ministries, Robert D. Bullard, Paul Mohai, Robin Saha, and Beverly Wright. *Toxic Wastes and Race at Twenty: 1987–2007*. United Church of Christ, 2007.

Valentin, Benjamin. *Mapping Public Theology: Beyond Culture, Identity, and Difference*. Harrisburg, PA: Bloomsbury T and T Clark, 2002.

West, Cornel. *The American Evasion of Philosophy: A Genealogy of Pragmatism*. Basingstoke: Macmillan, 1989.

West, Traci C. *Disruptive Christian Ethics*. Louisville, KY: Westminster John Knox Press, 2006.

White, Lynn, Jr. "The Historical Roots of Our Ecologic Crisis." *Science* 155, no. 3767 (1967): 1203.

Zachariah, George. "Whose Oikos Is It Anyway? Towards a Poromboke Ecotheology of 'Commoning.'" In *Decolonizing Ecotheology: Indigenous and Subaltern Challenges*, edited by S. Lily Mendoza and George Zachariah, 201–18. Eugene, OR: Pickwick Publications, 2022.

Index